Acknowledgement

A special thanks to Felecia Hatcher-Pearson, author of
Start Your Business On a Ramen Noodle Budget

*You can only live on potential for so long....there will come a time
when people will require you to cash in on that potential, and,
at that time, your potential must produce profits.*

PETERSON'S®

RIP THE RESUME

JOB SEARCH & INTERVIEW POWER PREP

Torin Ellis

About Peterson's®

Peterson's®, a Nelnet company, has been your trusted educational publisher for over 50 years. It's a milestone we're quite proud of, as we continue to offer the most accurate, dependable, high-quality education content in the field, providing you with everything you need to succeed. No matter where you are on your academic or professional path, you can rely on Peterson's for its books, online information, expert test-prep tools, the most up-to-date education exploration data, and the highest quality career success resources—everything you need to achieve your educational goals. For our complete line of products, visit www.petersons.com.

For more information, contact Peterson's, 3 Columbia Circle, Albany, NY 12203; 800-338-3282 Ext. 54229; or find us online at www.petersons.com.

ISBN: 978-0-7689-4111-1

Printed in the United States of America

10 9 8 7 6 5 4 3 2 1   18 17 16

First Edition

Dedication

To My Father

You told me to work hard. I wanted to save you. More than anything.
Happy birthday—March 23rd, 1947–2016

TABLE OF CONTENTS

INTRODUCTION

By virtue of our presence, we've been granted the opportunity to live life, travel the world, and search for our passion. No matter our class or stature, no matter the circumstances experienced while growing up, no matter the challenges we've had or have to overcome, we are granted permission to pursue a full life just by our existence. We have the talent required to solve problems, to thrive, and to be of value to others. We were designed to leave our mark on the world. Over the span of 18 years, I have built an extensive footprint in the Human Capital space through career development boot camps, coaching, building diversity strategies, and actually recruiting high-performing sales, sales leadership, and technical talent. I have worked with thousands of candidates directly and indirectly. These experiences have all been part of my adventurous and interesting professional pursuit toward a full life.

In 2015, I was asked, "Torin, after all these years of doing what you enjoy, what was the one thing that led you to come and share with others what you have experienced?" It seemed like an easy question to answer, but it actually challenged me. Considering I was on stage as part of a panel, I didn't have a ton of time to marinate, so I quickly provided an eloquent response that captured the attendees' attention. The panel ended on a high note, and, in true fashion, I left the people in the room with a clear understanding of my passion for the subject of career development, diversity, and parity around access to opportunity. Some time later, I thought about the original question and decided to share a more detailed response below. Have a look:

> **Question:** "Torin, after all these years of doing what you enjoy, what was the one thing that led you to come and share with others what you have experienced?"

Response: "I began to reflect back on all that life has afforded me. I have traveled to thirty of the fifty states, plus Japan, the Philippines, the Bahamas, Mexico, London, Paris, and Turkey, and I have met some of the most amazing, brilliant people. I have been a part of many life-changing speaking engagements with Monster.com (Making College Count and Making High School Count), the Maryland Business Roundtable for Education, and of course, on my own. I have hosted and produced several technology events on college campuses that attracted hundreds of high school students interested in learning about the power of technology and mentorship. I've had a magazine, a radio show, and explored gamifying the job search process. I've developed television and web series that address the career search and highlight the lack of diversity and have constantly explored how I might innovate in this space."

These are all contributing factors to why I decided to write this quick reference manual of job search and power prep tips. Pulling from each experience listed, I recognize that I hold a wealth of information and wisdom gained over the course of my own professional journey. To let all this remain tucked away either within or on a hard drive is a disservice. The timeline has been long in the making, in some ways overdue. Truth is, after three years of learning the recruiting ropes and engaging with tenured talent, I saw that many were unprepared for the interview process. These were professional men and women with five plus years of experience, earning $100,000–$200,000 per year. In addition, after hosting several events on college campuses and interacting with undergraduate students and recent alumni, I came to learn they were woefully unprepared for the job search and interview process. This was the case for several reasons, primarily youth and lack of experience, bad advice, and limited access to resources or understaffed career centers. That was back in 2001—now fast forward to 2016. In this economic and political climate, with disruption and innovation barreling down upon us, I know that you cannot afford to be ill-prepared in today's job market.

I believed then and believe even more now that my work is not in vain. In the midst of everything, I have made up my mind that no crisis will uproot my anchor, which is to be of service. My passion for the Human Capital space is deep, and I'm committed to leaving candidates and clients with a better recruiting experience. I still see the need to be of service to millions of alumni, undergraduate students, and tenured professionals alike. *Rip the Resume* is a digestible approach to having a sound job search and resume-development process. This guide serves as a foundation for your career growth today and tomorrow.

You can be told all day long *why*, but if you don't have the element of *how*, you will be stuck in neutral. Holding *Rip the Resume* in your hand was not made possible by one thing, but rather through the perseverance that I learned and applied in my life to constantly keep going in the midst of whatever was thrown my way. I experienced that economic collapse of 2001 (Internet) and again in 2008 (housing) and watched recruiters who had been in the industry for years run for cover. It made sense—they needed to generate income and provide for their families; in some ways, I should have done the same. Instead, I stuck with it. I continued to nurture my craft; I took the bumps and bruises of being shut out, shut down, and even told to shut up. I prevailed!

I encourage you that no matter what you are experiencing, if you believe in your preparedness and the mission, and you feel you have the resources to push forward, then do so. Enjoy this book and remember it doesn't stop here. Visit and interact on *www.riptheresume.com*. Follow me on social media. Encourage others to do the same. My purpose is clear: to deliver a resource that assists you in creating a new chapter in your life. I came here to break new ground and provide wisdom that is instrumental in building, cultivating, and helping you broadcast yourself. Let's RIP!

"As a six-year-old boy standing on the couch at my parent's house in Ohio, I wanted to own my own garbage company. I vividly remember throwing all my Tinker Toys on the floor and then jumping down to put them all back on the couch. To me, I was a garbage man and I loved it."

CANDIDATE FOUNDATION

1

STRAIGHT TALK

I could cautiously ease into the importance of building and maintaining your personal and professional (P2) brand. Delicately split the differences between products and services, highlight business models from logos we love and are learning to love and how their brand-building process is different from the one you will employ. I could drag this out for the next few paragraphs, but my style dictates a faster pace, so I'm not about to switch up now. I'm going to maintain my real-life persona, the person who thousands of candidates have grown to appreciate, depend upon, and respect. The guy who won Top Recruiter, Season 4, *Reign of the Bosses*. I'm going to be that guy who takes the ENTIRE job search, interview, and onboarding process SERIOUSLY. So let's hop to it.

The importance of personal brand building cannot be overstated. It precedes your foray into corporate America and displays in many ways your core character. Your personal brand tends to influence how your professional brand is erected and actually starts forming well before graduation. For most, the act of nurturing the personal brand happens and refines over time. For some, it is viewed as a fad, less than serious, and given reckless attention, if any attention at all. You can identify members of this group by their actions, their social media posts, their approach to course work, work-related opportunities and tasks, or just life in general. Thankfully, that last group is a small contingent and, hopefully, you are NOT counted in that number. You will hear the word *brand* spoken of often in your personal and professional life, so now is not too soon to suggest its importance, which is why I refer to it as a P2 brand. The phrase is so commonly used, but what does a P2 brand really mean to you when it comes to other areas of your life, such as landing a job, being in a position to achieve a promotion, preparing for a huge assignment overseas, or equally important, working with a local nonprofit to better the community?

The biggest challenge for most people working toward building their individual brand is lack of clarity. I've seen people excel and thrive in the community, professional, and volunteer marketplace, even without clarity. However, once you recognize that there are many elements that go into creating a recognized, reputable, and referred-to brand, you'll sustain an ambitious momentum and result for a greater period of time across a wider path of opportunity. In an ever-changing marketplace, you must be clear on and define what a P2 brand means to you.

These elements include having a thoughtful approach, a "doing" mindset, a spirit of growth, and a posture of developing others. Successful people recognize the challenge of how to combine these elements (and more) into who they strive to become. It's exciting, happens over time, and should be a process that is never finished or ignored. I remain in P2 status, except for when I run to the market wearing sweat pants with bleach spots and a discolored sweat jacket. My daughters remind me that I'm not living up to the fashion brand! That grocery store run is totally different, but image also contributes to your P2 brand, so in some ways my daughters are correct.

You are at a pivotal phase in your life, where it is paramount to transition from what you have always done to doing what is unfamiliar to you. I know this because you are reading this book. Let's face it: there are too many people who have the capacity to change the game; they just don't show up because they are complacent. You *have* to show up if you want to control your growth and outcome. Throw away the mentality of going through the motions; escape the mindset of complacency mediocrity. That space is crowded.

As a matter of fact, much of my achievement is a direct result of my hustle, from people recognizing my "get-it-done" approach, and therefore giving me opportunities that might have otherwise passed me by. How do you go from the usual to breaking out of the box and going after all that lies ahead of you? You think strategy, take action, take notes, recalibrate, and do it all over again. You do what the ambitious, the determined, the motivated do from time to time: they take risks. You have to be a dreamer who rises with unwavering commitment to aligning action with your thoughts in order to make things happen. Notice, I didn't say *for* things to happen but rather to *make* things happen.

Being self-aware positions you to continue building your P2 brand and skill set required to pursue and earn future opportunities. When you take advantage of these opportunities, you'll start to showcase your unique value proposition, and that will start to open additional doors. Faster. The pace of access is different for each individual, so do not measure yourself by someone else's timeline. Always go hard, show up, and leave it all on the field, as they say. Just protect your P2 brand in the process.

" All of your life experiences—whether positive or negative—have had an overall impact on your P2. **"**

CONCEPT OF P2

A brand can mean a number of things, but just what is a brand when it comes to you? P2 is the means by which you market yourself to others by bringing awareness of your unique accomplishments, attributes, experiences, qualities, and traits. We are all uniquely designed, and those differences allow us to offer something that no one else can.

Forget the idea that your brand should exactly mimic what everyone else is doing or be shaped in the likeness of the person to your left or right, or of the person you met on the train last week or saw onstage during a recent speaking event. You can blame social media for that "like me" trend. I see the same things you see from time to time. Most images or posts you will see as you scroll that small mobile screen resemble a scene from a blockbuster movie, another $5,000 vacation, or the latest episode of ratchet. Occasionally you'll bypass an image with a glimmer of education, good hope, and motivation in between. I'm not bashing social media, but, for the most part, it is used for entertainment.

Because we have more than enough entertainment, I do promise to keep this book 100 percent real, so that you have a road map to your version of professional success. So no flashy cars, no images of red bottom shoes—just straight text that assists in building a better you. You are an asset looking and working to be discovered, which can actually happen as a result of social media. (We'll talk about that toward the end of the book and maybe once or twice in between.) What sets you apart from every other candidate is your P2 brand.

The truth of the matter is that you are more than capable of smashing barriers, erasing boundaries, and achieving new accomplishments by simply ensuring that you do not abandon your authentic characteristics. All of your life experiences—whether positive or negative—have had an overall impact on your P2. The places to which you have traveled and the people you have met along the way have touched your brand. Even the education and training that you have been fortunate enough to receive have played an integral part in shaping who you are and how you communicate, process events, set strategy, establish tone of action, and evaluate outcomes. Take some time and really think about how you are perceived by others. This will help you to understand the concept of P2.

Despite all that you have been told, when it comes to P2 branding and its potential, you must be aware that a brand takes consistency and time. This is a process, requiring moving parts, contributions, experiences, failures, and results—all suggesting that the brand is something you have to construct.

- First, take your values, accompanied by your passions, to devise a plan that will target your audience. You were created to solve, revolutionize, and change something.

- Second, conduct a self-evaluation of your character so that you can strengthen your skill set and qualities. Bring everything to the table, and begin to fine-tune your strengths—and be honest about your opportunity areas.

- Third, uncover how to relate to and connect with people you are trying to influence. Enjoy life, get out there, and meet new people. Expand your territory and align yourself with people who are completely different from you.

JOB DESCRIPTION

COMPANY RESEARCH

Rip the Resume is about building a stronger candidate, which forces me to write with clarity and logical direction. Everything that I am sharing addresses the various aspects of a job search and interview scenario and is setting you up for success. Grab the seeds of my experiences and plant them into your routine immediately. As you practice more, you'll not only be better prepared but also be in a better position to spot the lead interviewer in group sessions or to be in tune so as not to let the conversation become derailed when the interviewer is not prepared. After this read, a better job search and interview experience will unfold.

It's important that you know that no one needs to give you permission to get creative when it comes to identifying potential opportunities. Don't just rely on the familiar company names; be willing to consider startups or working abroad for a few years. This may be an ideal time to experiment and carve out your interests, so that once you reach the five-year mark, you are closer to knowing that you are in a field that aligns with your passion.

For now, let's begin by identifying industries and creating a list of companies that fall within those industries. From your list, start with your top three picks that line up directly with where you are trying to take your job search. After you do this, you can start to review job descriptions on job boards, aggregators, career portals, and social media sites. Please, DO NOT be the job seeker who is just randomly applying for jobs. That strategy is a waste of time and prolongs your job search. It also increases frustration—yours as a candidate and mine as a recruiter.

There are four elements that I want to build upon:

1. **High-flying job description**

   For starters, a high-flying job description provides a snapshot of the company culture and a vision. Its rigid list of job requirements is a mission waiting for a superhero to solve it. High-flying job descriptions stand out by creating excitement, offering interesting responsibilities, and highlighting a path of growth and opportunity. They tend to be clear, concise, and touch on community engagement or industry impact. Most important, they suggest to you, the candidate, that if you take this role, you will increase your Monday morning excitement level. If it doesn't do that, it's not a high-flying job description.

2. **The mission**

Look for job descriptions that align with who you are and what you are able to bring to the conversation. It may not explicitly say, "what can you bring to the table," but it most likely lists a series of reference points as to the type of person the company is looking to hire. Your contributions should complement the mission. For example, former teacher Jess Gartner determined she could be more of a force outside of the classroom and launched a company after her stint in education and Teach For America. She decided the mission for her fast-growing Baltimore-based company would read as follows: "At Allovue, student success is the bottom line." At the San Francisco-based organization CODE2040, started by Laura Weidman Powers and Tristan Walker, the mission reads, "CODE2040 is a nonprofit organization that creates programs that increase the representation of Blacks and Latino/as in the innovation economy." If the mission doesn't resonate—you couldn't care less about student achievement or underrepresented groups—then you should reconsider if the job description is the best opportunity for you to pursue.

3. **70/30 alignment**

Now that you believe you have an opportunity tailored to your P2, it has to align with your skill set in a convincing, but not a complete, 100 percent way. Being excited about a potential job is one thing; being able to perform is completely different and most important. Over the years, I've noticed that hiring managers will make exceptions for certain characteristics they want in a candidate. So I stress to my candidates to follow the 70/30 strategy when evaluating a role. If you are not able to do 70 percent of what the position requires of you, then this is not a good match and you should not apply. The remaining 30 percent suggests a knowledge accumulation will manifest over time, and that is a good thing. As a recruiter, it is my job to make sure that you are not missing the nonnegotiable, must-have requirements, but the 70/30 rule is a safe barometer.

4. **Candidate communication**

You have established a stable foundation, and you are ready to thoughtfully start applying. Don't rush through this process. Ensure that you allow ample time to complete the application process free of errors and mistakes, that you express yourself with complete thoughts, using "you" and "laugh" rather than "u" and "lol." This point is important because, in this world of social media and text messaging, far too many applicants make the mistake of using digital abbreviation in a process that is still analog in evaluation.

#1 SECRET TO INTRODUCTIONS

I'm giving you the honest truth when I say that many people prevent themselves from achieving results because they simply do not go after what they want. Make sure you take this next statement as an operational mantra from this day forward:

"ALL THE EXCUSES IN THE WORLD WILL NOT ALLOW YOU TO SKIP TOMORROW, AND DOING WHAT OTHERS RESIST DOING WILL BENEFIT YOU." ~ *t:ell*

My position in building star candidates is that you must step outside of the normal flow of what EVERYBODY else is doing. Sure, it's risky. But I'm not talking about breaking the law. I'm initiating a more aggressive job search. For example, most career coaches, consultants, and job descriptions default to "apply online."

Why? Because they want to minimize their interaction with candidates, letting the system filter and sort. How does that help you? Big question. The bigger question is: how many who apply online, following the directions, are still waiting for a response? Any response. Exactly.

For star candidates, I suggest an alternative action that too few young people embrace. The #1 secret to the introduction is to pick up the phone and make contact. You are looking for an edge, and grabbing a person via live contact presents that opportunity to gain a jump on the competition.

Here is how you do it. Contact the company and ask to speak with the hiring manager or the person responsible for the job posting or the position of (fill in the blank).

Mr./Ms. (fill in the blank),

I noticed you are looking for (fill in the blank), and I was hoping you might share your direct e-mail address.

I know the position requests that I apply online, and I will gladly do so. I would also like to directly share my credentials for your review.

This ensures that I receive consideration and do not fall victim to being one of 400 other people applying for the same position sitting in the company ATS.

If I'm one of the 400, there's a good chance you may never see how much of a match I am and the immediate value I offer to the role.

ATS stands for applicant tracking system, which we will discuss in Chapter 7. I suggest taking this risk to avoid being one of the herd that applies only online and never hears back from the employer. Keep in mind, there are plenty of well-qualified candidates who meet the majority of the qualifications and never hear back from the employer. Not because the person possesses a lack of qualifications, but because the employer ran out of time or for some other reason was unable to personally review ALL online submissions for the position.

Do you want to be one of those that were overlooked? Of course not, which is why I suggest you pick up the phone. Making a phone call that includes the sequence of statements provided gives you the opportunity to actually compete and quickly establish rapport within five minutes. If the person on the phone refuses to share an e-mail address, you simply apply online. No harm, no foul.

Pay close attention to the language I used in the example. You DO NOT want the employer to assume that you are not able to follow instructions or that you are a person who operates outside of the boundaries or that hiring you today may be a problem tomorrow. Be sure you are fully prepared when you make the call. The hiring manager may shift into interview mode without warning, so you must be in a position to maneuver the conversation accordingly.

MOBILE MAKEOVER

Wait just one second. I can sense your excitement is elevated from finding a high-flying job description. Your level of expectation has increased from the feedback that you received after following the #1 secret to introductions. And now, I know you want to hit "post" on your social media feed to let everyone know what has just happened, but I have to stop you. Yes, discard that post. Not because the post is bad, but the moment you tag the employer, it expedites their attention to your social media presence, and you need to make sure your house is in order.

We have all heard the saying that first impressions are everything. That is true, not only in the physical aspect, but in the world of cyberspace. You click "send," and in a matter of seconds what you post has traveled around the globe and back again. You must be aware of what you are posting. Potential employer feedback or securing an interview may not be something you want to share at this moment. I'm not saying it's bad; rather, I'm expressing the importance of thinking before you decide to post or share anything on social media. Yes, social media is a great tool. Remember that you are representing your P2 when you are sharing information and that what you post has the potential to bring immediate attention to your brand.

There was a period of time in which job seekers presented a resume to companies that was heavily relied upon to determine if the candidate was a good fit. That has changed. Now, through the use of social networks, companies have ready access to a lot more information regarding you than ever before. Through the employment process, companies are able view information that you may think is hidden, allowing them to learn more about you, including aspects of your personal life. You do not want to eliminate yourself from the hiring pool because of social content shared that puts you in a negative light.

Sites like Social Assurity help you build and maintain a digital reputation. It is important to know what is under your name. In a time when modern technology continues to make enhancements, hiring managers, human resources, and recruiters are looking at the digital footprint you are leaving with the messages and pictures you are sending. Social Assurity understands that social media is a tool for showcasing all facets of life and that some people operate with no filter. It exists to help you build and protect your online brand. For some of you, it might be time to start posting purposeful content to build your professional online presence.

For example:

- ☑ **On Facebook:** respectable posts that show you having fun in the office, during your free time, or in the community

- ☑ **On Facebook:** informational or motivational posts that advance or uplift the reader or showcase industry awareness

- ☑ **On Twitter:** links to articles, market data, and information that show an employer you are aware of the space

- ☑ **On Pinterest:** infographics or other images that highlight your hobby or industry

- ☑ **On Instagram:** inspirational quotes, jokes, and other easy to digest media that is in good taste

Some of the items below will immediately disqualify you from consideration.

- ☑ Derogatory, inappropriate, and unprofessional pictures, videos, or information, including your screen name

- ☑ Affiliations with drug and alcohol misuse, and criminal activity or involvement of any kind

- ☑ Negative commentary about past employers or disclosure of confidential information

- ☑ Discriminatory verbiage about race, gender, physical ability, or religion

- ☑ Links to questionable content posted by others that includes sexual and/ or violence-related content

I am speaking not only about posting these things yourself, but also about allowing them to be posted on your networks or sharing or engaging in a way that implies your support of such topics. The same information applies to any websites that you have.

For instance, when my team searches for talent, we view blog posts and sites like PIPL, White Pages, and Whois, along with a list of other online destinations. You might have a personal blog that has nothing to do with your professional life. If it hits my radar, as a recruiter I take it into consideration, and it becomes a factor in how I evaluate you as a candidate. Anything online that we can attach to you as a candidate and have a high sense of confidence that it belongs to you is fair game for consideration.

The previous list of bullet points above tend to be NO CALL BACK bullets. And understand, as a recruiter, I'm able to see or uncover much of this by using your e-mail address. Yes, the one you have listed on your resume. Surprise! I know that this is eye-opening, and it should be.

When you broadcast the following (and similar) items on your personal site(s) and/or social media footprint, you gain interest with companies and organizations:

- ☑ Background information that authenticates your position or title within an industry

- ☑ A professional image that might resonate with viewers and not cause them to question your professionalism

- ☑ Displays of your creativity and interests in ways that highlight your potential contribution and personality

- ☑ Effective communication skills in written descriptions, avoiding "text talk."

- ☑ Awards and achievements, particularly those that emphasize your professional capacity to deliver results

Perform a digital name check or work with a professional firm like Social Assurity to assist you with this exercise. Go through everything you find that has your name on it and verify the information reflected. When necessary, declutter and delete, and reshape the desired profile or social media platform to match and represent your P2.

"A fun job required me to wear a snug-fitting pink polo shirt and brown apron while scooping ice cream for Baskin-Robbins. One of the best and most rewarding jobs that offered one of the most life-shaping experiences."

RESUME DECONSTRUCTION

2

I knew that after a few years of seeing one poorly constructed resume after another, something had to change. Despite the fact that books have been written and that templates exist, there are still too many candidates using poorly developed resumes. With the employment market seeking creative talent with an awareness of technology of some sort, the "oh, it's just a resume" posture will not make the cut. My whole mission is to kick-start an excitement around the process—an excitement that leaves you as a star candidate.

There is not one person on the face of the earth who would rebuff the opportunity to do something that they have always dreamed of doing if the opportunity and timing were right. Yet I've encountered more candidates than I can remember who have been in a position to pursue those dreams but lacked the motivation and will to execute the action the situation demanded. You might say they were content—or worse, scared—which I've also seen. You'd be surprised how many people are afraid to pursue anything beyond complacency. Once the opportunity is lost, the defeatist "It is what it is" talk sets in, and they assume the "this is the best it's going to get" posture. What a disappointment. You have to get solid in where you are so that you can keep climbing.

> **"** The fact of the matter is that there is no one right way to write a resume, just one thousand ways to write the wrong resume. **"**

When you are passionate about where you are trying to go, you will overcome barriers to arrive at your desired destination. You will do whatever you have to do to see to it that you go after what is yours.

It all starts with our minds. I could devote this entire book to addressing what your resume needs, but if you don't get your mind right to receive the information, then your resume will just stay the same. Mental stagnation can cause you to lose out on progress and time. With a clear and open mind, let's tear down the old document and explore the pieces necessary to reassemble a stronger resume.

When you mention the word *resume*, you open the floodgates of advice regarding length (One page or four pages?) and styles (Chronological? Functional? Targeted? Perhaps a combination?). If you talk long enough and to more people, they will show you countless examples that offer advice about blocking, color schemes, fonts, and borders. It can be a bit overwhelming. The fact of the matter is that there is no one right way to write a resume, just one thousand ways to write the wrong resume. My goal is to help you to develop a well-drafted document that will open the channel of communication between you and prospective employers.

Over the years as I examined one resume after another, I realized that a fresh perspective was needed. I felt enough "how to" models had been written and that the space needed a book resource that did more than piece together the components. I decided to speak to the person and the process, to connect with my clients as we moved together towards completely dismantling their resumes. I took this approach knowing that in the end, the resume would be reassembled and thoroughly examined and my clients would also discover a new way of thinking in the process.

Look at some of the reasons why resumes need to be deconstructed:

- ☑ Applicants submit entry-level resumes for executive- or leadership-level jobs.

- ☑ Obvious and longer than justifiable timespans are missing from resumes.

- ☑ Bullet points of information are included that have no relevance to the applicant's previous job.

- ☑ Vital information that would give the applicant an advantage is nowhere to be found.

As you can see, there are numerous areas of opportunity for resumes. A compelling resume is not something that you just throw together. (We'll look at this from a different angle in the next chapter.)

SCRAP THE UGLY TEMPLATE

Let's get to work on being seen. With the potential of hundreds of resumes being attached to each job announcement looking for talent, you need your document to stand out. A resume symbolizes you; it serves as an extension of your P2. *Rip the Resume* provides the infrastructure you need to build a career around. At the core of your process sits a resume. I want to spend some time painting this picture so you understand how crucial your resume is. I believe it is very important to share with you how so much happens before you dive into your resume.

First and foremost, be prepared to have to invest in your resume. People see the word *invest* and shut down almost instantly. It's too bad because it is the truth—you *must* invest. You are going to spend either money or time, and perhaps both. You can find a cost-effective professional resume writer or company that specializes in producing a top-quality resume and that's okay. I am not telling you to go broke trying to create a resume, but what I am telling you is that you have to get away from the generic templates that do very little to portray you as a formidable candidate. Those templates lack the sizzle.

Using boring and outdated templates, referring to books from five years ago, and consulting with people who do not interface with hiring managers and recruiters will have you racking up dollars and time in this process, neither of which will be well-spent. Saving you from a frustrating and potentially expensive exercise in futility is part of the reason I created this affordable and current resource. *Rip the Resume* tracks the needs of the current job market and forecasts what you can expect over the next two to three years.

If you want to go the professional route, it may cost you between $200 and $600 for a resume package. You can also do it yourself using the methods and real examples provided in this book. The resume is a critical marketing tool and should be sculpted in a unique way that attracts attention. Use the tools that are available and save yourself time in the process. Scrap the ugly template, digest the provided tips, and then assemble a winning document that shines!

3 COMMON MISTAKES

Before I touch on the three common mistakes, I want to state again that resumes should be error-free and presentable. Even today, sentence structure and spelling errors are still happening frequently. Many resumes are also missing pertinent information or contain gaps in employment. (A gap is usually defined as a period longer than six months.) If you want to minimize potential red flags when the hiring manager or recruiter reviews your credentials, make sure these deficits are not in your final resume. On the other hand, work history that is significantly outdated (longer than 15 years ago) or highlights from your high school career would probably not be relevant to the work you're doing or are seeking to do, so you can skip including that information.

In addition to the above, there are three common mistakes that require a bit more effort to correct but make a huge difference in how you present yourself on paper.

COMMON MISTAKE #1: INCLUDING AN OBJECTIVE SUMMARY

Unless you are being guided and nudged by the—and I mean *THE*—hiring manager for a particular job, using an objective at the very top is a thing of the past. Objectives are a poor use of space and reveal very little about you as a candidate and what you offer. Objective statements are often too vague to say the least. (This may have been the most important reason to scrap the ugly template to begin with.)

Most objectives are simple: "To find a company that will use my skills to grow the company and allow me to be a contributing member of society." To most recruiters, they are a way of saying, "There was no thought put into my resume, and I am just looking for another job." People use the objective summary to tell the company what they are looking for. No company needs you to tell them what you are looking for, but rather they need to know how and why YOU are the candidate THEY are looking for.

REMEDY #1: PROVIDE A PROFESSIONAL SUMMARY

Your mission is to gain interest in the mind of the people reading your resume. A well-written resume will have a professional summary or synopsis as the starter. This summary asserts your value, indicates what you can bring to a company, and entices the reader to investigate the remaining content. It will add an immediate difference in your presentation on paper.

Professional summaries highlight you. You are trying to attract attention, to be seen as the only one. Remember when you were the first to have the latest American Girl doll or to get a Segway hoverboard on your block, and when you went outside to play, you were the cool kid everyone wanted to be around? Similar sentiment applies. Your proper and strong use of the professional summary has the potential to make you that cool kid again. Use it as a way to sell yourself, so you get the buy-in from the company that you are the best person for the job. You are the one the company wants to be around.

COMMON MISTAKE #2: OMITTING VITAL DETAILS

Candidates do not provide enough detail about achievements or problems solved in previous roles. Sure, you supervised, but how many employees did you supervise? How long did it take you to solve that scheduling problem when the team was short on headcount? What were the measurable results of the department's implementation of a solution you suggested or an action you took? This kind of detail provides substance for your resume. This kind of detail separates star candidates from average candidates.

You can look at most template-based resumes from top to bottom, and the only numbers included will be those in the month/year column. Resumes that do not provide details of measurable performance achievements leave me and others like me to guess how effective a candidate was in the role. Don't make me guess.

REMEDY #2: INCLUDE THE NUMBERS

A resume should have numbers and show what you did while you were employed at various jobs. No one should be left guessing how much money you saved the company. Let the numbers show what you did. If you managed 20 people, state that. Get specific in detail, so there are fewer questions regarding your capabilities.

You can use numbers to address head counts, team members, staff support, patient counts, number of interns, size of summer camps, number of calls made, patients seen daily or weekly, or miles traveled. There are limitless examples of how you might categorize your contribution and participation while in a role. The challenge is to force yourself to do it when most will ignore the value of including this vital information.

Numbers mean everything on a resume. It should be informative and have enough detail to show what you did. At the same time, don't fabricate numbers.

COMMON MISTAKE #3: REPEATING INFORMATION

Resumes are boring if they just repeat from one line to the next something that has already been stated. This happens frequently when a resume is written by a novice or without creative energy and dedication, such as if a person with a history of similar jobs copy and pastes a job description from a company website, unaware that the description is identical to another listed on the resume.

I get it—flipping burgers is flipping burgers. Stocking shelves at Company A is the same as stocking them at Company B—I get it. But I challenge you to subscribe to a deeper thought, cultivate an open mind regarding the nuances of the role, and then succinctly share them in your resume. Star candidates do this—here's how.

REMEDY #3: USE SPECIFICS TO TELL YOUR STORY

While I don't need a resume, I invested 17 hours in developing a solid document that I review once a year. I want to always make sure I'm a superhero on paper. You must also be that superhero we spoke of in the first pages of the book. It's okay to use job descriptions that categorize previous roles you've had as a guide. Weave the wording into your account of the work you did, and develop a strong portrayal of your time with said company. You can use job descriptions from the exact company, or you can select the same title from a competing company.

Just a word of caution: Everything you put on your resume will have to be substantiated. Don't take shortcuts and try to shuffle your way through this process. It is not hard or out of the ordinary for hiring managers and recruiters to perform reference checks EVEN BEFORE you are ever contacted. There are calls that are often made to previous employers to see what kind of employee you were. Be honest with yourself. Integrity is everything when companies are trying to find the best employee.

Keep in mind that there is no need for five different versions of your resume. My philosophy is that when you develop multiple resumes, you inevitably leave out bits and pieces of who you are. I've seen people create multiple resumes: one for painting, the other for baby sitting, another for accounting, and yet another for event planning. I'm left wondering, "Who are you—professionally?" Get it together. You need one resume, and that is it. If you need to slightly modify your presentation, do that. But if you need to develop a completely different resume, then it is highly likely that you are applying for a role that is not a good match for who you are, despite the number of jobs you've had.

5 ADJECTIVES

Let's talk about the modifiers known as adjectives as they pertain to your resume. Their importance runs deep in terms of developing and telling a captivating story that results in getting an interview. Far too often, candidates undersell themselves or come across as average or uninteresting, which factors into how they are evaluated.

When considering adjectives, remember your audience and what they are looking for in a candidate. The job description and your research on the company have given you two pieces of the puzzle. Knowing the values and concerns of the company you want to join helps you tailor your writing in terms of the length, the quality of details to be provided, and the most effective examples to use.

As you start to draft your resume, you will be tailoring your message to resonate with one or more people. Your message has to speak clearly to their desired result(s), excite their creative meter, and calm their concern around professional matrimony. Put another way, convince them you would fit in with the other team members and hit the ground running with minimal disruption to the mission.

Your resume is a snapshot of you. Approach your resume the same way you live your life. Use a combination of nouns for persons, places, or things. Back them up with adjectives that describe and tell more about the nouns. Then add verbs to show the action and adverbs that describe your verbs. Sounds elementary, but the formula for writing a resume is unlocked with illustrative storytelling. You have to paint a picture—I refer to this as *artistical encoding*. Your words deliver an image, and hiring managers or recruiters find themselves imagining you in a previous role delivering a result or, better yet, as their employee helping them to grow their bottom line.

As a quick exercise, jot down five adjectives that best describe you in the space provided. Then write a complete sentence, one for each adjective, in a way that describes your professional persona. Use the examples as guides. Be specific.

5 Adjectives That Describe Me

Example: *Ambitious*

1. _____
2. _____
3. _____
4. _____
5. _____

5 Descriptive Sentences

Example: *Ambitious recent graduate who operates with focus and patience as an individual or as part of a team.*

1. _____

_____

2. _____

_____

3. _____

_____

4. _____

_____

5. _____

_____

39 ADVERBS

Writing a resume takes planning and requires attention to detail. The details are unlocked by the words that you choose. Routine responsibilities are amplified by the use of descriptive words that enhance your contribution statements. Well-chosen adverbs will illustrate and describe how you were able to accomplish, diffuse, engage, invigorate, or steady a situation. They are important as you shape the body of each work-related role you've held or volunteer activity you've participated in. Adverbs add the glamour that hiring managers and recruiters are searching for as they scan your two-page document. Adverbs differentiate you from a person who copies and pastes a job description from a website without modification. Well-developed contribution statements enrich your resume and represent you as an individual who presided over the resume-crafting project with attention to detail and personalization.

I've included a list of 39 strong adverbs to jump-start your options. Why 39? No reason other than I figured as a millennial, you'd get tired of reading a longer list. Refer to this page when you sit down to actually reconstruct your resume. Don't get carried away. I've seen candidates use wording on their resume that they were unable to elaborate on when challenged or queried. Knowing that you too will be asked about the smallest insertion on your resume, be honest.

39 Adverbs

Accurately	Dependably	Professionally
Actively	Diligently	Proficiently
Aggressively	Directly	Realistically
Ambitiously	Effectively	Regularly
Analytically	Efficiently	Reliably
Artistically	Energetically	Responsibly
Assertively	Enthusiastically	Significantly
Clearly	Independently	Steadily
Competitively	Intelligently	Substantially
Confidently	Logically	Successfully
Consistently	Passionately	Supportively
Courteously	Patiently	Technically
Creatively	Precisely	Thoroughly

5 ACCOMPLISHMENTS

Leave it to social media, and the prevailing notion is that EVERYBODY but you is balling. (I bet my editor is looking up the word BALLING right now trying to figure out what it means.) Truth of the matter is that while the streak of success portrayed on social media may be true, there is also another side to a professional career: the missteps, missed assignments, being late, and a list of other unflattering happenings exist as well. And just as most people decide to omit them from the many posts on social media, I suggest we do the same regarding your resume. This does not suggest you shy away from sharing those instances when you missed the mark or learned a hard lesson. It's just better to do that in person or via a phone call when you have more range to tell a complete story and potentially gauge the recipient's disposition.

The resume is where you brag!

Treat your resume just like others (and you) treat social media. The resume provides plenty of open space for you to dictate how your determination, efforts, and hard work allowed you to be where you are. The resume is your celebration of sorts, a time capsule of accomplishments that when opened by the right employer, is like a wish come true. The resume is a big deal.

Your resume is not just a piece of paper that lists tasks that you completed at your previous jobs. It is more than just what qualifies you for the position; it is your entry ticket to a conversation regarding your future. I'm going to assume you want your best *you* present for that conversation. You have gone through all the necessary processes of getting your resume in tip-top condition, so now it is time for you to step it up another notch and bring the proof of your accomplishments and achievements. This is not difficult.

The easiest way to do this is to think back to what previous employers have said about you during your reviews. We all have room for improvement, but what were some of the strengths that they told you about in that setting? Start piecing those together and retrace your past roles. Whenever someone has taken the effort to make you aware of something that you did, it is an accomplishment and therefore noteworthy.

Companies want people who can deliver. You are not a number. You are a human being with the ability to be more. Every individual, regardless of background or place of origin, wants to have a sense of accomplishment in his or her life; some just have to dig deeper to pull out the story. This is an important step, perhaps *the* most important one, in the deconstruction phase.

This is where you will spend quite a bit of time tearing down your resume and preparing it for reconstruction. This is your brand we are speaking of here. Accomplishment and completion are key indicators that the company can rely on you to get the job done. Since you are the one the company needs, you will have three accomplishments or achievements throughout your resume.

Challenge yourself to dig deep and find a minimum of three and no more than five powerful achievements that will broadcast who you are. These accomplishments will be listed under each role with the respective company. Then examine them closely, and spend some time on how you were able to accomplish each one.

Accomplishments

1. _____

2. _____

3. _____

4. _____

5. _____

If you need more room to fine-tune your accomplishments—or any of the lists in this chapter—take advantage of the NOTES section at the end of this book.

My father ALWAYS told me to work hard. He instilled in me that no matter what I was doing—from cutting lawns and shoveling snow to playing sports—just work hard. He was not one to welcome a list of excuses.

3

BIG PAPER

I'm a veteran of the United States Air Force. I chose that branch because at the time of enlistment, every branch paid the exact same amount, roughly $660 per month in compensation. For me, it was a simple decision: there was no reason to go through thirteen weeks of basic training "trauma" when I could do six weeks instead. To me, it was just dollars and sense. I didn't know when I enlisted, but in every branch of service, every enlistee is assigned an occupation. So although my job in one of the other branches may have been different in nature, each branch—Army, Navy, Air Force, or Marines—had the same mission. We had a duty to protect and to serve—similar to how I am looking out for you.

The standard was set, and we took care of business. Now with Form DD-214, my discharge paper, in hand, I'm holding big paper. I once protected and served, and this piece of paper proves it. The paper reminds me of how important it was for me to do as assigned, to collect intel, be analytical and communicative with my superiors, keep order, and remain protective of our air space. Every mission was a building block. While your mission is different, it is important that you nurture a similar mindset as you approach professional growth.

> " The resume is a collection of sequential activities, directives, meetings, missteps, projects, results, and trainings. "

You have to believe and act, knowing that big paper (resume) composition builds over time. This requires more than that familiar phrase "just follow your heart." Far too many undergraduates and recent alumni are holding firm a fresh degree yet are clueless as to how to move the process forward. They struggle with reaching out to employers and quickly learn that life happens fast—and it hits hard, too. Connecting the dots of life from chapter to chapter requires plenty of effort and a plan *and* a dose of "just follow your heart." I went from high school to the military to Corporate America, and every transition required a different formula. There is no difference when it comes to the process of becoming a star candidate. Life becomes the front line, with building big paper as the mission.

The resume is more than just a piece of paper. The resume is a collection of sequential activities, directives, meetings, missteps, projects, results, and trainings. Every experience is preparing you with a transition lesson in life. Things happen, but your responsibility is to uncover why. The lesson within the experience is what you must capture. A solid resume serves as an entry point to that first conversation. NOTHING happens without a conversation, and your resume has to convince human resources, the hiring manager, or recruiter that allocating 30 minutes to an hour of time is something they should do.

Your attitude means everything. It is how you approach a particular scenario—for instance, how you engage with a superior or manager when he or she is having a bad day. Or your ability to interact with an overly aggressive and dominant peer, or your flexibility when your schedule is upended when other team members check out on a critical project. All of these examples share how you develop big paper. You will manifest reference-worthy results by remaining focused on the end goal and being able to document your actions over time.

Maintaining that focus will trigger those star candidate qualities. Star candidates not only create big paper but also shine in the transition. Growth requires EVERYONE to work; some work harder, but all have to put in work. No one has all the answers, but you'll benefit from the experience in each event, moving closer to doing what you were built to do, and building a paper footprint worthy of congratulation and compensation. Put another way, big paper!

PROFESSIONAL SUMMARY

The requirements when it comes to your resume were touched on briefly in Chapter 2. It is necessary for the next sections to be broken down further, so that you properly construct a resume that allows a person to scan it and say, "Now here is some TALENT!!!" Screening potential candidates should not be complicated when it comes to the first glance. Your personal professional summary should leave the hiring manager or recruiter looking to connect with you to discover more about you.

This section of the resume serves as the headline. Refer to this section of your resume as the marketing narrative, summarizing a brief account of your personality through your qualifications, which, in turn, introduces who you are and highlights your skill set.

Take a look at a professional summary statement that has traction. Increase the impact of your professional summary statement by selecting effective words NOW!!

Professional Summary Example:

> *Successful top-producing mortgage specialist with over 10 years of residential and commercial real estate experience. Managed a medium-sized asset protection firm ($500k book of business), achieving substantial financial returns for all clients by implementing personalized financial risk portfolios. Leader in growth and development of five business partnerships by providing strategic client-specific training processes.*

This summary creates a spark in the eyes of human resources, and the hiring manager or recruiter, and it encourages them to take a closer look to see what this individual has to offer. Notice, there is no ambiguous language. It is clear what the candidate can do. The adjectives are incorporated throughout the summary. The relevant numbers speak to the capacity in which the candidate is able to operate. The candidate maximizes his or her expertise and makes achievements known.

After you have written your professional summary and begin crafting the body of the resume, make sure that the declarations you have made in the summary statement can be validated by the hiring manager or recruiter. You might insert a few key core competencies you possess like the ones below:

Key Core Competencies Include:

- ☑ Personalized residential and commercial portfolio development

- ☑ Proven financial asset building and forecasting using statistical data

- ☑ Professional business development strategies and training

Both the professional summary and the bulleted competencies (optional) were concise and related to each other. It was done in sync, and one spoke back to the other. Now that is how you *Rip the Resume!*

3 VITAL ASPECTS OF RECONSTRUCTION

By now you've most likely grabbed your laptop and started to reconstruct your resume. That's a good thing, especially if you believe in trial and error, moving things around, or simply jumping in and giving it a go. The way this book is written lends itself well to you putting the covered material into immediate action. As you approach this section, pay particular attention to 1) the use of numbers, 2) aesthetics, and 3) colorful, descriptive language. Done right, you'll have an end product that reads beautifully, tells a story of growth and production, and serves as an invitation to a conversation.

As reconstruction is underway, refer back to your professional summary so that you connect those top line statements to internal content and reflected contributions. You want the reader to learn about you effortlessly, feel wrapped in a balanced display, and not have to guess as to how one thing connects to another. Remember, recruiters don't spend a great deal of time on the resume, so if we can't connect your experience to the opportunity quickly, we move to the next candidate. In order to show congruency, every section must be aligned and cohesive in thought so one part complements the other.

1.   **Using numbers when describing duties, leadership, responsibilities, and results is essential.** Numbers are definitive, and, when used, they tell a reinforced story. The numbers you include on your resume have to be authenticated. Be certain the numbers used can be proven by you or by the contact person for your reference checks, or by a reviewer with intimate knowledge of your previous employer or industry. For instance, I have seen candidates removed from the process because their dates didn't match up during the reference check.

The numbers that you want to include in your resume are:

- ☑ Numbers that show increase in terms of growth: How much new business was generated? How many new clients were acquired?

- ☑ Numbers that show savings or profit: How much in revenue did you help bring in? How much money did you help save the company as it relates to cost?

- ☑ Numbers that show a span of time or a range: How long did it take for you to accomplish this? Exactly how long were you in a specific role?

You are looking for numbers that demonstrate. It might be a challenge to have actual numbers throughout your entire resume. That is all right. Use them where they will fit best. The resume does not need to end up looking like you just left algebra class and are trying to show the recruiter that you know how to solve an equation. The right numbers will show what you helped produce and problems you helped solve within the company. The numbers matter and rightfully so, because they show what you accomplished while you were employed.

2. **Presentation and overall readability are important.** Include indicators that speak to creative experiences and/or solutions you bring to the organization. I call these indicators *power statements*. Power statements highlight details of completed tasks, experiences with the public, challenges overcome, and the like.

The more descriptive you are with your statements, the easier it will be for hiring managers and recruiters to give the resume proper attention. Keep in mind, the suggested standard for a resume review is under 60 seconds. Power statements are personal and should be treated with care, which is why a few are placed at the very top. Be mindful of the need to strategically place your power statements, similar to the ones used in the professional summary. The presence of power statements keeps the reviewer's attention as he or she transitions through your document. Treat each power statement as a formal introduction between you and the reviewer.

3. **Use of colorful, descriptive, and rich language substantiates results.** Presented right, your personal story takes shape and turns into big paper. It's okay to discuss challenges you experienced on the job. If you go this route, just be sure to show 1) that you grew through the challenge, and 2) how you've positioned yourself to overcome such challenges in the future. Be aware that there is limited space when crafting these micro-stories into a solid document. Be confident in presenting your whole self. You'll learn more of how to do this when we hit the section about the interview.

Again, it all comes back to knowing that you are worthy of securing what you desire by backing up content with action statements, production results, and/or problems solved. We have all done great things. Just supply the information so that the right set of eyes can pick up on these great attributes and say, "You are the one that we have been searching for."

COLORFUL LANGUAGE AND PHRASES

Let me illustrate and reinforce the power of colorful and descriptive language. The main reason that I had you make that list of adjectives was so that you might incorporate them throughout the resume. This step must be embedded in the reconstruction process. Without it, your resume is flat and lacks vibrancy.

Take a couple of minutes and see if there's a description that fits you among the examples below. If so, great—incorporate it into your resume as a gift from me. If not, perhaps the phrases used will inspire you to craft a colorful description of your own.

Expertise in training and mentoring inexperienced analysts, creating developmental timelines, and documenting progress.

Superior emphasis on business development, market penetration/expansion, and customer service w/more than nine years of Sales Management experience.

Teamed to deploy, as well as maintain, a comprehensive suite of innovative mobile solutions at the University of Maryland Eastern Shore.

Tasked with cold calling accounts that were nonresponsive to or not interested in advantageous refinancing alternatives offered.

Arranged critical and team-building conference calls and assisted team members with a variety of administrative duties.

Demonstrated effective telephone and computer skills while providing timely and error-free service to customers in growing regions of the company footprint.

Confident and poised in interactions with individuals at all levels. Capable of quickly learning and applying complex concepts. Skilled in training, motivating, and supervising employees.

Highly engaging communicator and connector focused on the Sales and Sales Leadership discipline across various industries.

. . . .

Offered individual motivation and sales strategy based on need. Reversed the productivity of multiple low-ranking teams, resulting in sizable increases in productivity and revenue.

. . . .

A consensus builder and servant leader adept at building high-performance teams that continue to deliver amazing results in a crowded space.

. . . .

Maintained a self-directed process of inputting critical data used to measure inventory, deliveries of new merchandise, and generating reports.

Descriptive phrases help paint a picture of the essence of a person. The resume has to be bursting with colorful phrases and words to make that possible. Create this document in such a way that it is your official marketing mouthpiece. This is *your* story. Take the reader on a journey of your accomplishments, background, skills, and tenure by using descriptive phrases and key words that provide glimpses of an effective candidate.

BEFORE AND AFTER SAMPLES

When I started *Rip The Resume*, I wanted to make sure that value was built into every aspect, whether the downloadable PDF or an in-person career development boot camp. In order to assist those who like to do things themselves, I had to include a few before-and-after resume examples. I decided to go the extra mile and showcase examples that are worth $200 to $500 in terms of professional assistance. See what improvement ideas you can glean and incorporate as you reconstruct your own resume.

SAMPLE 1

This particular resume was very plain and unappealing. I worked with Chris Fields of Resume Crusade to develop a better presentation for this confidential candidate, whom we will call Chris Smith. In your review, you'll notice the wording is uninspiring and doesn't share what this person has accomplished. It's simply a collection of duties.

CHRIS BEFORE:

1. Heading is boring and flat; it includes different font sizes, which portrays as lack of attention to detail.

2. Overall format is linear and uninspiring—nothing about it (excitingly) invites a deeper review.

3. The use of *Responsible* for and *Ensure* is not as potent as stronger words like *managed* and *created*.

4. General information like typing, WPM (words per minute), high school graduation date, general skills, and customer service carry little importance.

1

Chris Smith
8889 Bristol Lane
Memphis, TN 38112
(C) 901-555-5555
chris@costofwork.com

Work Experience

Corrections Corporation
Administrative Clerk *March 2013—Present*
- Order and receive supplies and equipment utilized in the ongoing operation of the facility.
- Type memorandums and official documents using computer-related programs.
- Oversee, supervise, and assign work to inmates assigned to a designated department.
- Maintain inmate accounting records and deduct charges from inmate trust accounts.
- Update inmate files with confidential information using web-based documentation.

2

The Funeral Home
Human Resources Asst *February 2012—Present*
- Process payroll and approve time sheets.
- Administer compensation programs and monitor employee evaluation programs.
- Interview and select most qualified candidates.
- Maintain compliance with federal and state regulations concerning employment.
- In state employee incentives to boost staff morale.

Corrections Corporation
Sr. Inmate Counselor *June 2012 to March 2013*
- Resolved daily inmate issues and staff issues before they became significant matters, incidents, or grievances.
- Responsible for services and programs delivered to inmates assigned to designated units.

3
- Reviewed KRONOS time sheets to maintain staff punctuality in regards to their assigned posts.
- Processed payroll for inmate workers under direct supervision.
- Provided direct supervision to a staff of 25 or more Correctional Officers in the facility.
- Ensured that unit sanitation was upheld by unit staff and inmates.

Corrections Corporation
Corrections Officer *July 2011 to June 2012*
- Maintained order and provided security in a corrections facility.
- Provided care and direct supervision of inmates and residents.
- Maintained unit sanitation standards.
- Oversaw daily operations while supervising 300 inmates in a corrections facility.
- Enforced rules and regulations while being a leading example for inmates.

Technical Skills

4
- Microsoft Office 2011 Applications: Project, Excel, Word, and Power Point.
- Excellent typing skills (55 WPM).
- OMS-Offender Management System to input inmate data.
- TOMIS-Tennessee Offender Management Information System to input inmate confidential data.

Education

LaFayette High School
Honors Diploma Graduated May 2011

North Ashworth University
Associate of Applied Science; Human Resources Management (Expected graduation April 2014)

After interviewing the client, Chris Fields wanted to make sure the bullet points reflected the candidate's true performance.

CHRIS AFTER:

1. Updated heading and added certifications suffixes to the name to include the LinkedIn Profile link.

2. Moved the "Education" section with certification toward the top, adding value within the short professional tenure.

3. Updated the verbs on the opening statements and improved the sentence structure and language.

4. Anchored with a "Computer Skills" section to show relevance and close out the document with value—not another "references upon request" statement.

Chris Smith, SHRM-CP, PHR
8889 Bristol Lane ✛ Memphis, TN ✛ 38112

Linked **in** Chris Smith   ph. (901) 555-5555   ✉ chris@costofwork.com

Strengths

- Training and Development
- Recruiting and Hiring
- Workforce Management

- Employee Relations
- Employee Engagement
- Payroll and Compensation

Education
Associate's Degree in Human Resources Management, North Ashworth University (April 2014)
SHRM-CP, PHR, Society for Human Resource Management

Experience
True Label, *Recruiting Coordinator*   **Oct. 2014–Present**

- ☐ Oversee the continuous recruiting and hiring of temporary workers to fill entry-level positions
- ☐ Process and submit I-9s, healthcare deductions, garnishments, and other court orders
- ☐ Attend multiple college and job fairs; perform background and reference checks 10x per day
- ☐ Coordinate and organize the new hire training and onboarding processes
- ☐ Analyze and review exit interview data monthly to identify areas of employment improvement
- ☐ Propose additional HR structures that are successfully implemented into policy

USPS, *HR Assistant*   **June 2014 –Oct. 2014**

- ☐ Coordinated and processed all new hire paperwork for the unionized labor workforce from I-9s eVerify, wage garnishments, and other court orders
- ☐ Arranged new hire training sessions and onboarding for all workers increasing efficiency by 12%

The Funeral Home, *Human Resources Assistant*   **Feb. 2012–May 2014**

- ☐ Worked with HR Manager regarding payroll, compensation, FMLA, LOA, and healthcare benefits
- ☐ Managed employee paperwork for compliance purposes, e.q., medical, tax, and contact info
- ☐ Processed I-9s and W-2s for all employees, garnishments, and other deductions
- ☐ Assisted with recruiting, interviewing, screening, and hiring of new employees
- ☐ Updated and maintained training material, employee guidelines, and manuals
- ☐ Reviewed and approved time sheets, paid time off, sick time, and medical leave
- ☐ Created a quarterly employee recognition program to boost morale and participation

Corrections Corp., *Administrative Clerk*   **March 2013–May 2014**

- ☐ Oversaw administrative duties for the Federal Prison under the U.S. Marshals
- ☐ Processed inmates accounts, financial records, packages, mail, and other official documents

Sr. Inmate Counselor   **June 2012–March 2013**

- ☐ Managed the daily workload and whereabouts of 25 Correction Officers throughout the facility
- ☐ Investigated and resolved problems with inmates, de-escalating matters and maintaining peace
- ☐ Reviewed and approved timesheets in KRONOS time tracking and payroll system

Corrections Officer   **June 2011–June 2012**

- ☐ Enforced rules of the prison system, maintained order, and provided security
- ☐ Supervised 300 inmates during visitations, meal periods, exercise, and recreation times

Computer Skills
Microsoft Office: Word | Excel | PowerPoint | Project | Kronos

All resumes are different and are influenced by the career field, level or tenure, and position held. The combination of these factors dictates a lot of the design process. The next three samples illustrate how resumes can be arranged to present strong candidates with varying levels of work experience, education, and area of expertise.

SAMPLE 2

This resume represents an undergraduate student still enrolled in school who has secured one internship.

CHRISTINE BEFORE:

1. Educational experience, although important, hijacks valuable space.

2. Layout suggests a general resume—a collection of courses and odd jobs.

3. Date stacking (Month/Year) on the far right is confusing to the reviewer and the Applicant Tracking System.

4. Portrait of experience lacks any one or two instances of achievement or success.

Christine Jones

111 Old Trace Dr. | Raleigh, NC 27611 | (901) 555-5555 | christine.jones@email.com

EDUCATION

North Carolina State University	**May 2015**
B.S in Business Administration	
Concentration: Human Resources	
Dean's List	**Fall 2013**
GPA: 3.50	

RELEVANT COURSE WORK

Related Course work: strategic staffing, training & development, compensation systems, interpersonal communication

Course Projects:

- Created a Recruitment Plan by conducting a job analysis, writing job descriptions, creating advertisements, and identifying target markets for Lakeside Hospital on their strategic staffing system to determine supply and demand.
- Conducted field research and analysis on the health benefits package of Seaboard Hardware in a team of six that included design, implementation, and PowerPoint presentation.
- Conducted field research and analysis on the Employee Development Program at Seaboard Hardware in a team of six that included design, implementation, and PowerPoint presentation.

LEADERSHIP

President, NCSU Society for Human Resource Management	**May 2014 –Present**
Liaison and Team Leader, North Carolina State University	**Aug. 2011–May 2012**

EXPERIENCE

Tutor and Mentor   **July 2010–Present**
- Working with 10 students in grades 1–8 in Mathematics, Reading, Writing, and Spanish
- Providing weekly assistance in subjects that need improvement
- Creating projects and assignments
- Providing one-on-one tutoring sessions at clients request
- Planning and chaperoning local field trips
- Arranging meeting agendas and guest speakers for "Girlie Talk Org"
- Scheduling monthly meetings to review productive study habits

Administrative Secretary, All Impressions, Raleigh, NC   **Apr. 2009–June 2010**
- Responsible for creating a welcoming environment for clients, ensuring great customer service
- Scheduled 20+ follow up appointments weekly for clients
- Maintained a periodic inventory system of 50+ products
- Organized and restocked inventory monthly
- Trained 3 employees to keep inventory

SKILLS

- Leadership & Communication: Ability to share knowledge and encourage others in order to achieve specific team goals while actively listening and asking relevant questions
- Systems Knowledge: Familiar with Microsoft Office Word, PowerPoint and Excel
- Problem Solving: Ability to work independently as well as with others within the organization to find the most efficient solution to the current problem and produce quality results within the allotted amount of time
- Record Keeping & Organizing: Ability to balance work, provide team support, and perform personal responsibilities in a timely and professional manner. Ability to keep organized records and note special details

ACTIVITIES

Deliverance Cathedral
- Volunteer during the summer to assist with TLC Vacation Bible School

Since there is not a great deal of work experience to present, this resume focuses on the candidate's strengths and accomplishments to highlight her potential for growth and future success.

CHRISTINE AFTER:

1. Added a "Profile" section—more specific and valuable than an Objective.

2. Hybrid resume style combines academic and traditional elements.

3. Added a "Strengths" section, which adds context to any candidate—especially one with limited experience.

4. Anchored resume with "Education" and "Professional Development" sections to close on a solid point of reference.

1

Christine Jones

111 Old Trace Dr. ✣ Raleigh, NC ✣ 27611 ✣ christine.jones@email.com ✣ ph. (901) 555-5555

Profile

Currently enrolled at North Carolina State University earning a Bachelor's Degree in Business Administration with a concentration in Human Resources Management. Pursuing an HR internship/entry-level position to gain experience and real-world knowledge.

2

Strengths

Human Resources Fundamentals | Recruiting | Compliance | Leadership | Critical Thinking |
Employee Relations | Compensation | FMLA | EEO | ADA | Healthcare Benefits

3

Experience

U.S. Equal Employment Opportunity Commission (EEOC)   May 2014–July 2014
Enforcement Supervisor/Investigator Intern
- ☐ Worked closely with the Area EEOC Office Director on various projects, active and pending cases
- ☐ Investigated cases of protected class discrimination; Age, Sex, Race, and Religious complaints
- ☐ Conducted 9 interviews with Charging Parties and Respondents for evidence and information
- ☐ Drafted 10 case responses utilizing HR insight and facts from investigations and interviews
- ☐ Performed HR data analysis regarding employee demographics, compensation, and benefits
- ☐ Provided administrative support as necessary to the full-time Investigators and Director
- ☐ Trained new interns on policies, procedures, and onboarding of the EEOC organization
- ☐ Successfully lobbied the Director to reopen a case against 2 experienced Investigators

Tutor/Mentor   July 2010–Present
- ☐ Tutor ten (10) 1st – 8th graders regarding Mathematics, Spanish, Reading, and Writing Skills
- ☐ Create weekly assignments and projects for practice and improvement
- ☐ Coordinate and arrange the itinerary and agenda for "Girlie Talk Org," including guest speakers
- ☐ Plan and chaperone local field trips, arrange meetings, and review study habits

All Impressions, *Administrative Secretary*   Aug. 2009–May 2012
- ☐ Greeted clients, made appointments, managed schedules, and provided superior service
- ☐ Maintained and tracked inventory control systems with over 50 products
- ☐ Trained new employees and provided additional assistance as necessary

Major Human Resources Projects

- ☐ **Created a Recruitment plan for Lakeside Hospital strategic staffing system; conducted a job/work analysis, wrote job descriptions, created advertisements**
- ☐ **Collaborated with 6 team members to develop a Healthcare Benefit analysis and an Employee Development Program with field research and analysis for Seaboard Hardware**

Education

Bachelors in Business Administration – Human Resources, North Carolina State University
(May 2017)
Dean's List Fall 2013| GPA: 3.026

4

Professional Development

President, NCSU SHRM (Society for Human Resource Management)–Current

SAMPLE 3

This candidate, although lacking a great deal of work experience, possesses many desirable skills; however, the resume lacks focus and obscures her professional identity.

DAO BEFORE:

1. Layout suggests a general resume—a listing of odd jobs and skills.

2. Portrait of experiences lack any detail around achievement, responsibility, or success.

3. Format is top heavy with a very weak closing—typical when one has limited work experience.

Dao Cuong
555 New Street, Apt. A
Baltimore, MD 21217
443-123-1234
DaoCuong@email.com

Job Description: I've excelled in meeting my entire sales targets for each day of business, as well as making my customers feel the most comfortable. I've demonstrated proactive duties within my work. I have proven my ability to multitask and get work done on or before schedule.

Overview

More than two years' experience in childcare, and more than a year of experience working for and managing fashionable boutiques and retail establishments in Baltimore, MD. Recognized for delivering outstanding customer service. A verifiable track record of success backed by impeccable references. Areas of expertise include:

1

- Exceptional Customer Service
- Merchandising and Display
- Childcare
- Microsoft PowerPoint

- Microsoft Excel
- Microsoft word
- Problem Solving
- Inventory and Pricing Controls
- Computer/POS Scanning Use

- Ability to work well independently and on team projects
- Visual Design

Employment

2

Harlem Park Recreational Center
Summer of 2010
Union Baptist Head Start
Summer Of 2011
Jimmy Jazz
6901 Security BLVD, Baltimore MD
SALES ASSOCIATE
2013–Present

Education

Western High School, Baltimore, MD
High school diploma
College: Catonsville Community College
2013–present
GPA: 2.3
Major: Mass Communication/English

Personal

Enjoy and active in:

- Journalism
- The Arts and Theater
- Poetry

- Dance
- Communication
- Blogging

3

The revised version utilized eye-catching design elements and specific details about the candidate's achievements to paint a clear picture of who she is professionally, even at this early point in her career path.

Dao After:

1. Used the top third of the resume to attractively display her experiences using more inviting phrases.

2. Added bold headings to shift the focus from her limited experience, so the reader can see the candidate in a different light.

3. Implemented the use of bullets to round out the bottom two thirds of the resume in a way that many hiring managers prefer.

DAO CUONG

555 New Street, Apt. A • Baltimore, Maryland • 443-123-1234 • DaoCuong@email.com

Key Strengths and Benefits

Exceptional Customer Service	*Merchandising and Display*
Inventory and Pricing Controls	*Computer / POS Literacy*
Consistent Team Player	*Documented Individual Contributor*

1

VALUE OFFERED

Results-Driven Professional: Exceeded monthly sales goals since start of employment
Problem Solver: Proactive and reliable member of the team considered self-directed
Customer-Focused: Capable of providing coverage and working with multiple clients

PROFESSIONAL EXPERIENCE **2**

Jimmy Jazz: *Sales Associate*   *January 2013–Present*
Increased sales production by 8%

- Met general daily procedures/sales; maintained quality customer service
- Counted money at the beginning and ending of shift to ensure accuracy
- Consistently recognized for exceptional service and professional work habits

Union Baptist Head Start: *Teacher Assistant*   *June 2011–August 2011*
Enhanced learning environment for students

- Proven ability to communicate to students and parents in a positive manner
- Substantial knowledge of child growth/development and behavior characteristics
- Kept teacher informed of particular problems of individual students

Harlem Park Recreational Center: *Team Colleague*   *June 2010–August 2010*
Demonstrated outstanding communication skills

3
- Proven ability to maintain an active curriculum in sports activities
- Extensive knowledge in self- and student organization
- Recognized as Colleague of the Month for outstanding performance and recommendations

Education: *Currently attending Catonsville Community College*
       Major(s): (a) Mass-Communications–(b) Business Administration

Extracurricular Activities:

The Arts and Theater • Journalism • Dance • Poetry • Blogging

LINDA BEFORE:

1. Heading is off-center, missing a line of separation; shows a lack of attention to detail.

2. Objective is less than convincing and serves as a poor use of space.

3. Opportunities are presented in reverse order, with oldest job shown first.

4. Bulleted items are presented with no color or life, just a routine listing of responsibilities.

LINDA BLOCKER

111 I Road–Baltimore, MD 21234–301-555-5555–linda-b@email.com

OBJECTIVE

To display a great deal of proficiency in machinery, customer service and team building by incorporating my training, knowledge, and experience in the work environment.

EDUCATION

Lock Haven University of PA, Lock Haven, PA
General Studies
August 1997–January 1999
Lake Clifton High School, Baltimore, MD
High School Diploma
April 1992–June 1997

PROFESSIONAL EXPERIENCE

Machine Operator, October 2000–August 2010
WorthWhile Armstrong Venture, Aberdeen, MD
- Maintained a clean and safe work area
- Ensured acoustical ceiling grid was produced within the specification guidelines in a quality form
- Trained new employees on producing acoustical ceiling grids
- Implemented safety training, machine training, quality assurance training and the company philosophy training in Pune, India
- Assisted with the start-up of a new branch of WorthWhile Armstrong Venture in Pune, India

Mentor, November 2012–March 2013
CBBT Inc., Baltimore, MD
- Monitored youth who had been ordered to take part in positive juvenile programs
- Maintained documentation that was processed and collected by the state of Maryland
- Stayed positive and was influential to all youth clients with whom I interacted

Transportation, August 2010–Current
Riding With Block Transportation, Baltimore, MD
- Transport clients to specified destinations in a safe and prompt manner
- Maintain a positive business relationship with the dispatchers
- Abide by all traffic laws while driving throughout the state of Maryland

AFFILIATIONS

Volunteer, Baltimore City Track & Field, Mentor, November 2010–Present
Volunteer, Pikesville Football, Mentor, August 2008–Present
Volunteer, Baltimore Celtics, Coach, November 2011–August 2012

CERTIFICATIONS /AWARDS

Certification of Completion, Maryland New Directions, November 2010
Certificate of Completion for Beginning and Intermediate PC,
Maryland New Directions, October 2010
Employee Council, WorthWhile Armstrong Venture, July 2008–July 2010
Perfect Attendance, WorthWhile Armstrong Venture, 2008
Employee of the Month, WorthWhile Armstrong Venture, October 2003

The revised version of the resume is bolder, and, while compact, presents a stronger candidate for consideration.

LINDA AFTER:

1. Updated heading and added separation lines to make the candidate's resume stand out.

2. Replaced the section highlighting a brief college stint with a more powerful Summary section.

3. Rearranged the bullets to read in paragraph form with two bulleted highlights under each role.

4. Anchored with EDUCATION and AWARDS/CERTIFICATIONS sections to give the candidate a solid, one-page document.

LINDA BLOCKER **1**

111 I Road • Baltimore, MD 21234 • 301-555-5555 • linda-b@email.com

SUMMARY

- Accustomed to operating equipment and machinery with reliability and zero incident rate
- Expertise in training and mentoring, motivating team members, and achieving timely results **2**
- Effective communicator, respected by peers, with a history of volunteer activities supporting youth

PROFESSIONAL EXPERIENCE

CBBT Inc. November 2012–March 2013
Mentor
Managed and monitored more than five (5) highly charged youth mandated to program participation. Worked with other team members to provide research, support, and training of critical mandates and programming. Collected data, compiled and used by the state of Maryland. Displayed positive respect so that youth considered me a go-to resource.

- Classified as the most reliable mentor for youth with adverse issues
- **3** Dedicated to work objectives, provided near 24/7 availability for youth of the program

WorthWhile Armstrong Venture October 2000–August 2010
Machine Operator
Consistently produced acoustical ceiling grid with quality in a safe manner. Maintained a clean and hazard-free work area. Ensured that acoustical grid was developed using specific guidelines and quality considerations. Trained new employees based on my tenure and unblemished work record. Performed troubleshooting of mechanical issues that impacted production.

- Selected to launch an international location in Prune, India
- ZERO reprimands and absenteeism of less than .5% during ten (10) year tenure

EDUCATION

Lock Haven University of PA, General Studies   August 1997–January 1999

AWARDS / CERTIFICATIONS **4**

- Certification of Completion, Maryland New Directions (Nov 2010)
- Certificate of Completion for Beginning and Intermediate PC, Maryland New Directions (Oct 2010)
- Perfect Attendance, WorthWhile Armstrong Venture (2008)
- Employee of the Month, WorthWhile Armstrong Venture (Oct 2003)

RUSSELL BEFORE:

1. Tenured candidate presents a flat introduction in the first 30-second review of experiences.

2. Display lacks alternative use of color†, fonts, and lines to enhance reviewers eye movement.

3. There is no use of numbers that scream accomplishment or production, which is always a red flag.

4. Skill Highlights section is weak when you consider the tenure of the candidate.

---

† Although not visible in this publication, well-placed splashes of color can set a candidate apart. See the "Russell After" list for suggested locations of color to this resume.

Russell J. Reynolds

Address Information Confidential

EXECUTIVE PROFILE

1

An accomplished and imaginative executive, committed not-for-profit leader and regional director with a flair for successfully leading change. A consensus builder and servant leader with particular emphasis on training, developing, and motivating others. Strong background in managing budgets in excess of $40 million. Experienced in strategic planning and growth management. Adept in all aspects of event planning ranging in attendance from 50 to 4,000. Accustomed to delivering results.

4

Effective Communicator	Budgeting Expertise
Project Management	Customer/Stakeholder Focus
New Product Development	Strategic Planning
Community Engagement	Human Resources Trainer

PROFESSIONAL EXPERIENCE

2

Regional Publisher, 10/2009 to 02/2015
Confidential Company

3

- Recruited to provide vision, leadership, and accountability in eight markets. Oversaw all aspects of business operations, including effective P & L management.
- Accurate forecasting and budgeting, business and new product development, talent management, and community relations.
- Led the consolidation of 30+ publications from thirteen graphic design/ production sites to two centrally located hubs resulting in significant cost reduction.

Director of Development, 04/2007 to 10/2009
Confidential Company

- Designed and facilitated the curriculum for an internal leadership development program (Leadership Institute), an annual ten-month program providing comprehensive training in communication, conflict management, public speaking, team building, and other essential leadership components. Responsible for teaching multiple sessions as well as the coordination of outside instructors. Worked directly with CEO to provide programming that strengthened succession planning initiatives.
- Designed, coordinated, and facilitated customized training sessions and workshops based on enterprise-wide needs assessment.

HONORS AND AWARDS

- Indiana Commission for Women Torchbearer Award in Media and Communications
- YWCA Salute to Women of Achievement Professional Award

Reworked, this resume showcases a tenured candidate who is complex and displays a vibrant collection of experiences in a style that will capture a hiring manager's attention.

RUSSELL AFTER:

1. Placed introduction on steroids—gave it pop quality, which draws in the reviewer.
2. Inserted distinct bullets that highlight candidate's range of responsibility within the first 30 seconds.
3. Expanded and inserted a new section that provided a visually stimulating display of the candidate's skill set.
4. Used color[†] and word font variation, added numbers, and closed with self-directed development.

---

‡ Areas where color was used on the finished resume: applicant's name; address information; boldfaced text in the professional summary; job titles; professional training titles.

Russell J. Reynolds...

Address Information Confidential

Widely **accomplished and imaginative executive** and change agent who accelerates corporate results among disparate teams. High emotional intelligence and personal accountability. Exceptional ability to engage and inspire others with a sense of urgency.

P&L / Financial Performance: Provided oversight of all aspects of business operations, including effective P & L management, accurate forecasting and budgeting.

- ☐ **Operational Excellence:** Led the consolidation of 30+ publications from 13 graphic design/production sites to two centrally located hubs resulting in significant cost reduction Improved employee engagement, reversed turnover, and improved trend by 3%.
- ☐ **Executive Leadership:** Worked directly with CEO to provide programming that strengthened succession planning initiatives.

Expertise that Creates Sustainable Business Results

☐ Staff Development / Motivation	☐ Executing for Results	☐ Project Management
☐ Alignment / Collaboration	☐ Change Leadership	☐ Budgeting Expertise
☐ Effective Communicator	☐ Cross-functional Team Leadership	☐ Human Resources Trainer

Vision and Strategy for Building, Protecting, and Strengthening Market Leadership

Confidential Company   04/2007–02/2015
REGIONAL PUBLISHER, 10/2009 to 02/2015

Developed vision, leadership, and accountability in eight markets. Led business and new product development, talent management, and community relations. Secured right-sized office space, finalized space plan, negotiated facility lease, and coordinated moves for nine business units.

- ☐ Provided planning and oversight of national internal leadership conferences.
- ☐ Deployed management and HR training for more than six (6) business units enterprise-wide.

DIRECTOR OF DEVELOPMENT, 04/2007 to 10/2009

Designed and facilitated the curriculum for Leadership Institute, an internal leadership development platform for promising talent. Combined educational components, speakers, and leveraged technology during an annual ten-month program providing comprehensive training in communication, conflict management, public speaking, team building, and other essential leadership components.

- ☐ Designed and facilitated numerous customized workshops based on enterprise-wide needs assessment.
- ☐ Identified key strengths and blind spots of each team and developed a process to maximize their potential.

Awards

Indiana Commission for Women Torchbearer Award in Media and Communications
Indiana Trial Lawyers Association Journalist of the Year
Indianapolis Bar Foundation Award for Outstanding and Unstinting Devotion to Community
Indianapolis Bar Association President's Award

Professional Training

Myers-Briggs Type Indicator Step II facilitator, 2011
Thomas Kilmann Conflict Mode Instrument facilitator, 2008

The *Rip the Resume* process highlights the glaring errors and edits that appear in many resumes, especially those that are done by the candidate or by others who offer resume writing assistance. The landscape has been reset and requires a shift from a casual approach to genuine dedication to the resume development process. In times of challenge, taking the path less traveled, although initially daunting, proves easier and far more rewarding in the long run.

It is no secret—none—that securing employment options for graduates will become even more challenging with demand shifts in the economy, off-shoring of jobs, advancements in technology, and politically charged regulations. Students will need more than a degree to compete against the next candidate.

Without fail, I constantly hear HR leaders and recruiters admit that the recruiting process inherently carries its own unique challenges. The truth is, more than you might imagine, there exists a gap in your ability to deliver a rich interview experience. This candidate gap exists for several reasons, and successfully closing it takes more than basic job search strategies and cut-and-paste resume styles.

Everything begins with understanding the magnitude of the gap and what it is that employers want, are missing, or could benefit from in order to render you as the ideal candidate. *Rip the Resume* is engaging, interactive, and results-driven, using real-world examples—not theory. It is designed to help you fill that gap. In the end, you will gain more when you invest more in the process.

Take some time now to digest and reflect on the resume transformations you've just seen. Use the following page to jot down ideas you might consider incorporating into your reconstructed resume. If you have a question about what works and what doesn't, feel free to contact me: **torin@torrinellis.com**.

NOTES

_____
_____
_____
_____
_____
_____
_____
_____
_____
_____
_____
_____
_____
_____
_____
_____
_____
_____
_____
_____
_____
_____
_____
_____
_____

I slipped up a bit, took my studies less seriously, and saw my grades suffer. While I carried a solid B average, I could have done much better. I could have positioned myself for scholarships and unfortunately didn't get to enjoy the college experience.

STAGE ONE— RECONNAISSANCE

4

Up to this point, we've covered many of the foundational aspects of becoming a star candidate. It was important to reflect on the process and think about who you are before you started working on the interview. It is due to a lack of foundation that so many candidates bomb the interview and extend their job search. You have the vital qualities to become a star candidate, so now we can explore stage one with increased confidence.

Reconnaissance is another word for *research*, and *research* is another word for *digging*. Average candidates use a big shovel to dig at this stage in the process. This poses problems. Star candidates dig with a spoon a little bit at a time and are much better at adapting their conversation because of their preparation.

Grabbing a spoon and gathering small pieces is better than trying to force the company research and job search preparation process all at once. Pay attention to all of the details as well as the process. *Rip the Resume* is written like a building block— one step precedes and is just as important as the next. Don't skip ahead and try to take shortcuts. Do your research on the company. When the time has been put in, it will show.

Everyone is all excited when getting a call to come in for an interview, whether with a recruiting firm or with the company directly. Granted, it is very exciting! Choose not to be just any regular candidate though. You've already researched the company you want to be a part of. It is just as important for you to familiarize yourself with the recruiting firm as any other objective that you have tackled.

Knowing that I represent both the candidate and the client shows that you took the time to research and find out about me, the recruiter. So, for instance, know that The Torin Ellis Brand is a human capitalist strategist, diversity ambassador, interview architect, and consultant to a number of well-respected brands and companies. That is just one part of it. Learn what the recruiter's level of expertise is. To be clear, my brand does all of the following regarding a candidate: coaching, sourcing and scouting talent, working with the media, participating on panels, and providing talent strategy services. It is an added bonus for you to know the relevance of the mission of my firm. We have a concentrated focus on diversity and inclusion and a profound respect for differences in perspectives, cultures, and overall life experiences.

How is knowing this information a step up for you? It prepares you to come well-equipped for the next phase in conquering the hiring process. Take the opportunity to seize all that lies in front of you. Do the research and learn about the business.

Everything that you have put in place to be successful just makes the conversation flow better when you do get called in for an interview. The meeting shouldn't feel like a deposition. Being a better prepared candidate leaves an interviewer feeling no added pressure because the interview is inviting and engaging.

Be familiar with the ebbs and flows of the market, so that you are well-versed. Always go a step further and speak with both existing employees and even those who have exited the company and get their perspective on things. Remember to be objective based on facts and not subjective based on feelings. Get a feel for what it is actually like to be operating in the capacity of an employee. Preparing well is all about entering into the interview having already done the work, instead of looking for work when you get there.

RECON-WEBSITES

True growth comes from stretching the boundary of familiarity, and you are already a step ahead of the game because you have put in the effort. Use your time to prepare for the interview by leveraging a mixture of technical platforms that are widely in use today:

IFTTT ALERTS:

Google Alerts keep you abreast of what is taking place in the industry. **IFTTT is the super power.** That may sound like a strange name, but for anyone like me who's in the customer relationship management (CRM) space, IFTTT stands for If This Then That. It's a workflow tool. Anyone can use it. Learn how it works and make it work for you. IFTTT is predicted to become the backbone of the next wave of Internet of Things technologies.

HOOVERS:

The thing that people commonly focus on is the company, but they do not have the slightest idea about the industry itself or where the company fits into the industry. Use Hoovers to access the largest commercial database of 85 million companies, 100 million professionals, and 900 industry segments; relevant social media links; and customizable news feeds.

DUN & BRADSTREET:

Unlike most data providers, Dun & Bradstreet is a content creator rather than just a data aggregator. Industry-specific business analysts compile unbiased insights on the top 43,000 global companies, including publicly traded and private ones. You can find reports on key competitors, financials, and executives in clear summary formats.

ZOOMINFO:

Sites like Zoominfo allow the recruiting process to be organized and streamlined by bringing the people puzzle together. Backed by a database that contains over 140 million businesspeople and 9.3 million businesses, Zoominfo's Growth Acceleration Platform dynamically puts professionals in position to identify, connect, and engage with qualified contacts. There is a paid version, but the complimentary version provides access to information that may be useful in the interview process. This is part of the star candidate's formula for uncovering who to approach and how. The *how* helps you meet the needs of companies and shape the conversation.

SALARY.COM:

I can attest to people showing up with no idea of what they have the potential to earn because they just accept whatever is thrown at them. Candidates of color and women suffer the most from being undercompensated in part because they do not negotiate or do not have the information that will equip them to negotiate better compensation.

Get acquainted with all the resources that are available to you and use them. One resource is the Salary.com Salary Center, where users can access in-depth salary information, read about ways to negotiate a higher salary, and map out their own path for capturing their full economic value at work.

CONVERSATION MAPPING

Hopefully, by now the core components needed for a successful job search have become relatively clear: the job description, your resume, and you, the star candidate. The phone will eventually ring, and you will find out how prepared the hiring manager or recruiter is for the conversation. Without question, you will be prepared. Distill your energy in a measured way, as you want to match the momentum of the caller. The process of securing employment is a combination of marketing, sales, and skill set review. How each part is weighed by the hiring manager or recruiter is outside of your control. The reason why we have touched on each aspect is to highlight the importance of each phase.

It is time for some coaching on conversation mapping. When it comes to interviews, most candidates are nervous, when in fact the interviewer is only looking to have a conversation. Prepare to have fun. Don't get me wrong; it is normal to be nervous. It comes with the territory. However, preparation tends to alleviate much of the stress, and I've found role playing works amazingly well at this stage.

" When it comes to interviews, most candidates are nervous, when in fact the interviewer is only looking to have a conversation. Prepare to have fun. "

Conversation mapping is another aspect that clearly distinguishes a star candidate from an average candidate. Star candidates use conversation mapping to maintain structure in the interview setting and help steer the conversation toward a favorable ending while taking note of pertinent information for later use. When I am interviewing for a client, I know what he or she is looking for, so my questions are tailored toward the needs of the business and mission. I ask questions that are relevant to achieving the desired result.

When more than one candidate is applying for the same job, my interview questions are consistent from one candidate to the next. That way, I'm able to evaluate the candidates as evenly as possible. In conversation mapping, the star arrives with an array of introduction options, transition statements, and questions to ask once the power shift takes place. Yes, the person asking the questions is in power. Interviews are meant to be positive interactions with all people involved, and that requires you to ask thoughtful questions.

There will be questions that will challenge you. They are meant to catch you off guard and force you to stall for a moment. This is perfectly acceptable, as most interviewers are looking for a slight pause in your response. Don't run and hide from questions that cause you to stop and think. It is not always about what you know, but often about how you react to situations that you are faced with. Don't try to run around the question, nor should you provide a superficial response. Star candidates own the conversation process and are able to authoritatively deliver a positive or negative response.

Never make the assumption that just because you have been interviewed many times the atmosphere will always be the same. Always take note of information that is being provided to you.

Interviews should not be difficult to conduct, nor should they cause individuals to second-guess themselves. The priority should always be to add depth in short bursts in order to make the conversation interesting. The reason that star candidates are able to arrive for the interview prepared and leave feeling accomplished is because they also take notice of the subtle things and are able to make them come alive during the conversation. They are not afraid to connect, speak up, and quickly build rapport. They add to the conversation. They aren't trying to hide anything. They are transparent and really put themselves out there. Star candidates are remembered when they leave.

ATTITUDE ADJUSTMENT

You know that your life is one big roadmap; use this to your advantage. You have to be ready at all times for situations presented. You can be the best at what you do and have everything working in your favor, but a true test of any person's character is the ability to adjust and press forward when the course bends. The unexpected curves and turns require a different response to the presented challenge. The unprepared and the very best alike must adjust to avoid abandoning progress.

In every area of life, embracing the adjustment so as to not repeat the same cycles over and over again is recommended. There is a season for everything that we step into. Everything that we go through, whether it be mistakes, flaws, setbacks, or defeats, has one thing in common: how you choose to respond to what happens to you is a big indicator of where you will end up in life.

That choice is dictated by your attitude and ensuing action. Star candidates recognize there is a race that has to be finished! Stopping before you make it to the interview, secure an offer letter, or receive login credentials is the equivalent of raising the professional flag of surrender. Challenges require a blistering belief in yourself no matter what you are experiencing, keeping a positive outlook, and maintaining character.

It takes a very disciplined and determined lifestyle to make it against all odds. Excuses are irrelevant. There will be challenges, delays, and tests, yet giving up should not be your most familiar option. You have to believe that your endurance will pay off. You have to become your own advocate. If something doesn't work out the way that you thought it should, go back and look at what did work, modify the shortcomings, and pursue a more favorable outcome. Be pliable and able to make edits where needed.

Many of you just need to be revived and reminded that you are on the right path or very close. Some of you might be trying to put all the pieces together, but, just as when solving a puzzle, simply need a different viewpoint. That is what this is all about.

We all have undergone challenges that have left us wondering whether we were going to make it. We all have trying days when we are going through different things, but we have to remain patient. There is no instant magic wand, and everything is built upon over time. The job-seeking process requires all of you and forces growth from learning the beginning and the ending of how things work together. Each action has what you need to move on to the next action.

Eighteen years is a long period of time in this industry. My experience has made it clear to me that many people do not embrace the seriousness of the job search. Sure, it matters on the surface; I mean, who doesn't want a paycheck? Achieving full and passion-filled employment for longer than 90 days is more than a paycheck. Approaching a job search as if it is a chore to check off is the reason why so many talented people find themselves just going to work and then quickly starting to search again for another opportunity.

Many candidates are nonchalant and rote going through the process of the job search, oftentimes completely disengaged. Usually a candidate's look or line of conversation tells everything before being asked one question.

There is nothing more dissatisfying than seeing people who have full-blown potential present themselves in a fashion that automatically disqualifies them. There is an aura of presentation associated with your brand. Being able to take responsibility for what you do have the ability to control starts with your attitude. Recruiters don't like to spend countless hours scouting talent to interview a candidate who portrayed one persona, only to then find out that the person sitting in front of them is a liability to their client.

Companies are looking for more than people who need jobs. Hiring managers and recruiters want talent that can join the business unit, department, or team and bridge gaps and solve problems within short days or weeks. Remember that industry standards suggest hiring a new employee is costly—and even more so if the employee has to be replaced—with some suggesting the cost is two or three times the annual salary. In other words, hiring is a critical and extensive process. As a candidate you need to do more than **casually** look for a job.

People are counting on you; that is why they invest in you. So much is riding on your candidacy in the job-seeking process. Star candidates will always have the best attitudes. Having the right attitude and bringing a high degree of interest in the role will allow the company to further grow its business. Ultimately, the people who work for a company will either push it forward or drag it down. Attitudes impact the culture of a company as well.

You know of people who often complain and are negative when they go to work each day. Think about how that impacts the overall morale of the organization and other members of the team. Any successful organization realizes that the people who are part of its team, the people it has invested in, are the number one factor of its success. Entailed in this process are the financial resources for training candidates and providing them with the necessary resources to do the job well. Companies lose money when the turnover rate is high. Looking for the right person is key to retaining the best talent. This is not about the revolving door mentality when it comes to companies.

Served my time in the military as a 202, a Communications Analyst, in the Philippines. Every day I was reminded of the the focus that Sergeant Cook demanded I develop and how important it was to be heard in your communication. To be clearly heard.

STAGE TWO— 5
THE INTERVIEW

WEALAE

During the hiring process, I have seen that much time is spent on generalizations of a candidate's profile that focus mainly on areas of strength. Cool. I've also seen a number of candidates, more than I can count, hesitant to address their opportunity areas. Everyone has strengths and things they are proud of, but they also have aspects of who they are that demand extra attention. Present your strengths and weaknesses via short stories. Maybe you are awesome at attention to detail, performing research, or uncovering a line of code that is hidden deep within a program. AWESOME. Be ready to tell your story.

On the other hand, your challenges might be administrative, in how you communicate, check your emotions, or maintain focus when the list of action items is long. It could be in following up, motivating others, or being hyper-competitive. We arrive at our destination, not by everything going right all the time, but in those moments where we have to strive to overcome obstacles that at first appeared as huge stumbling blocks standing in our way.

This book has been constructed in a way that develops you as a whole candidate. Remember that. I purposely did not insert shortcuts, because at this stage, it is important that you have a solid foundation. Truth of the matter is that uncovering and securing FULL EMPLOYMENT demands plenty of preparation, execution, and then some. If you don't believe me, ask one of the 1.8 million newly declared graduates in 2016 who are working for minimum wage. To that end, part of a winning formula in the job search and interview process demands that you arrive at your interview having already done the work, not looking for work.

I coach candidates using the WEALAE acronym. WEALAE stands for Wage Earner Act Like An Entrepreneur. Hiring managers and recruiters are looking for more than general statements and topical questions. They are looking for creative talent with experience or signs of talent that can quickly get up to speed and make an impact within the company or team. This requires more than simply validating the contents of your cover letter and resume. It requires that spoon I mentioned in Chapter 4. The WEALAE method allows you to demonstrate star-candidate qualities.

The theme behind WEALAE is that entrepreneurs, people who own their own business, tend to work much harder. In the beginning, they are responsible for multiple activities and various tasks both inside and outside of the business. There is no one to rely on, but the call still must be made. The books must get kept. Invoices have to be sent out and collected on. Internal bills must be paid, and on top of all that, new clients have to be generated. Entrepreneurs don't have the luxury of focusing on just one task. As a candidate, you are in a better position if you operate with the mindset of an entrepreneur.

Being an entrepreneur myself, I know what it takes to go from being hired to hiring, for myself and for a number of clients over the last 18 years. Now, as I build a dominant recruitment marketing and talent acquisition footprint, clients expect me to deliver "push play" talent on the first try. Sure, they'll give me another shot if I miss on the first submitted candidate, but they are unwilling to give me five, six, or seven tries to get it right. Recruitment is a blocking and tackling activity that costs each time it is done. Companies need and want to keep those costs as low as possible, and therefore, they want to hire the right person at the right time—the first time.

Throughout my career at companies such as MCI Communications, I acted upon what I saw myself doing. When I was promoted to a supervisory role and had the opportunity to hire telephone sales reps (TSRs), I always looked for candidates who displayed the qualities I displayed when I was a TSR. I knew that if I could identify assertive, confident communicators who were active listeners, I could turn them into selling machines. I was spot on in that my process helped me to develop a highly respected and high-performing team that was recognized as one of the best in the entire country. My character, my persona, who I am today as a professional started to form when I was young.

If you are serious about advancing your professional position, you will aggressively seek avenues that will take you there. Your internal drivers will kick in, and self-motivation will trigger your taking action and not waiting for someone to tell you that tasks need to be done. That spirit of living the dream will show in the effort you put in. Acting in this capacity allows you to have a long-term rate of return, instead of a reactive, now, "in-the-moment" short-term vision.

Again, sometimes, there are people out there who boost to the top quickly. This is a process, however, and it does take time. You have to want this. When you approach and use WEALAE, it really allows hiring managers to not suffer through the interview, but instead really find the quality of hires their companies and organizations so desperately need. You hold on the inside of you everything that you already are. It just has to be birthed and born. By transitioning the way you think about a lot of the things you have experienced in life, you will live out what you have always envisioned. There is something in each of us that we were made to do. It all starts with you.

" As a candidate, you are in a better position if you operate with the mindset of an entrepreneur. "

Come to terms and grips with the areas that are lacking in your life. Remember that an interview is merely a reflection of the overall view of who you are. The key to a successful interview is knowing you have a limited amount of time to convey a strong story that starts with the basics of who you are, has an arc that highlights your contributions and ability to be an asset, and provides a close that ensures the interviewer that you are the very best candidate.

You have to be able to articulate how you have been able to achieve your successes and what plans you have put in place to overcome and conquer your weaknesses. There are two sides to an interview. One the one hand, you have to be able to relate how your life experiences have helped you in your endeavors and how you can focus them on real job situations. Provide examples. On the other hand, areas of weaknesses will open the doors for you to speak to and relate to people who have faced similar challenges. Walk in your truth. There is something to be said for being able to announce that, yes, here is an area you need to focus on to become better. WEALAE!

OBSERVATIONAL LOGISTICS

Instagram. Snapchat. Vine. This is the era of now, fueled by applications that provide immediacy of the moment. Each application allows you to somehow be part of the moment, even if temporary. You are able to use your smart phone or other connected device to enjoy the moment. The core motor skill being used is observation, which is also required just before you begin your interview. Observational logistics use the same principles of immediacy. You have to be in touch with what is going on. Again, be present in the moment.

As you arrive on site, this is your signal to dial into another gear of preparation. Turn on your sense of sight and begin taking in the things you see around you. Notice, with purpose, the person watering the plants outside of the building or the parking attendant wearing a name badge and yellow ribbon supporting our veterans. When you enter the building, acknowledge the security guard, greet the person in the elevator, and pay attention to the building aesthetics. Before taking a seat, warmly greet the receptionist, provide your name (naturally), and look around.

Scan the area and take in small details of the office, flow of traffic, noise level, and mood of those present. Everything is a story and, at that moment, you are both part of the story and witness to it. The pictures on the walls, awards and plaques, mission statements, and other motivation suggest the culture. It might also suggest an angle of how inclusive the company is or needs to be. Yes, diversity is important! All of this observation is shaping aspects of the interview experience. Most immediately, it will impact your conversation.

Once you enter the office or conference room for your interview, be sure to recognize the mannerisms of the person you are interviewing with. As best you can and when appropriate, be prepared to emulate and extend the same cordial conversation using data points gained from the last 15 minutes on campus. Starting an interview with a reference to the weather is not a conversation starter. It might actually suggest a slow start or a boring interview. How did I arrive at that assessment? Simple. The lack of conversation has allowed me to form a negative opinion. That's exactly what happens at this point in the process: opinions are formed.

Your goal is to be interesting and to attempt to shape these opinions. Being conversational helps. People are more likely to hire people they like and can see themselves working with. A less-than-interesting or non-talker may not fit into the office composition. Use your observation to spark an interesting conversation, thus nurturing a desire in the interviewer to learn more about who you are. Be interesting and be eager to know more. No one goes through all the work I've presented in the previous chapters to simply arrive, answer a few questions, shake hands, and leave.

This is a time to open up and have a powerful conversation that will direct you on the path that you are on. As I am out in the field networking and meeting people, I am always looking for a way to share details of the moment, commenting on activities, people, or sounds around me. At the same time, I am observing the body language associated with people's responses, helping me to calibrate my next string of words. I'm in the position I hold today because of my keen ability to connect with people. Now, my family would argue that I'm not that way, because around them, I let them do the work. I'm … quiet (*smiling*).

5 SIZZLING QUESTIONS

Showing up to an interview and thinking that the interviewer is the only one who is supposed to be asking questions is not really an interview at all. Interviews are not one-sided. They are meant to be an effective two-way communication between people. How many times have you been on an interview and asked less-than-thoughtful questions that center on 1) days off, or 2) salary, or 3) the employee break room area. And before you ask, those are serious questions I have heard from both undergraduate students AND adults over the years.

If you focus on these topics, not only are you left wondering if you interviewed well, but you are also not being given any real detail that helps you make an intelligent decision regarding the company and/or team you are considering joining. The interview is not about just questions and answers. The conversation has to go back and forth with purpose. Asking questions really opens up the channel for communication to flow more smoothly. Once you have been given the green light to ask questions, be prepared to seek clarity and search for the details. This is where so many candidates drop the ball.

This is so important that I'm going to clearly list the format for the five questions you need to ask because you can't afford to get this wrong. Here they are:

TWO QUESTIONS THAT SOLELY DEAL WITH THE DUTIES ITSELF:

1. Can you describe for me an average day in this role?

2. How will I be evaluated in this role and by whom?

ONE QUESTION THAT UNCOVERS THE IDEAL PERSON FOR THE ROLE:

3. If you could hire ANYONE for this position (Athlete, CEO, Entertainer, Philanthropist, other), who would you hire and why?

ONE QUESTION THAT TARGETS THE GREATEST CHALLENGE(S) OTHERS HAVE FACED IN THIS ROLE:

4. Would you please share the top one or two challenges that have prevented others from excelling in this position?

ONE QUESTION THAT DRAWS THE MEETING TOWARD A CLOSE AND TRANSFERS POWER BACK TO THE INTERVIEWER:

5. Do you have any additional questions for me based on this exchange?

Your questions and the sequence are important. If done right, you will uncover the ideal candidate sought for the position, the reporting structure, and criteria for excelling. Before you leave, you'll have one more opportunity to become that person—if you really want the role, that is. Knowing just what the position is that you are applying for gives you a hint of what other people have had to face. Remember, the interview is almost over and you don't have a long time to authenticate the exchange, but you do have to act in a way that closes the conversation with the promise of being the best candidate.

As the interview starts to come to a close, the power will shift back to the interviewer to debrief with you. He or she will share insight with you. As it concludes, be sure to ask if the interviewer has any further questions for you. This will be a chance to reflect back over the conversation mapping and ensure that nothing was left out. Your next step is what seals the meeting, so pay very close attention.

TRIAL CLOSE

The conversation is nearly complete, and once you leave, anything can happen. The person or persons conducting the interview review and possibly exchange notes. Other candidates are given consideration. Some are lost in the shuffle of disorganization, applicant tracking systems, or because their interview was terrible. Whatever the reason, you want to make sure you leave the meeting as the star candidate. You want the decision makers rooting for you.

All of the responses that you gave during the interview should have been captured. Now you are following up to ensure that they were indeed captured, which is what makes the trial close so important. It is the one question, the only question that decisively places the interviewer(s) in a box. If you want to be taken seriously in your career, you need to learn now how to place the crosshairs of advancement where they belong. This interview determines if you advance to the next round, so make your mark.

Star candidates ensure with their actions that they leave a long-lasting impression. Consider how powerful it is to have the interviewer reflect on your engaging exchange, your demeanor and energy, your warm smile, and your powerful close after you leave. The interviewer nods in silent approval of how it all came together, knowing that your interview was the one that exceeded expectations. Place the pressure on the interviewer to provide a promising response by positioning a very direct question. You came to WIN! Wrap everything up and bring it all together with this:

"Given all that we have shared over the last hour, I'm now even more excited about joining the organization. Have I answered all of your questions completely? I don't want to leave you wondering if I am the best qualified candidate for the role."

Then you say,

"What's my next step in joining your team?"

Had to find my way. That journey included an on-the-job accident that almost cost me my life!

STAGE THREE— 6
THE CLOSE

"What's my next step in joining your team?"

The reason that star candidates are able to obtain what they set out to achieve is because they stay hungry from the beginning through the entire process. They're methodical and relentless, and they ask for what they want. So many candidates don't ask for the opportunity. I've called hiring managers over the years and learned in the feedback shared that well-qualified candidates lose in the decision-making process because they don't ask for the opportunity. They don't express an interest in wanting to be a part of the team. Believe me, decision makers want to hire people who want to be part of their team. This is the way you close an interview:

"What's my next step in joining your team?"

Throughout *Rip the Resume*, you have been presented with a wealth of my personal experiences, new processes, ways of converting things you already know, and a new way of thinking about the career search landscape. Be encouraged and continue to go further. Realize much time has been spent on making you aware of how to approach the resume and searching process.

Remember, it is never okay to just blend in. In order to achieve maximum results, you have to be a star. This is the same way of thinking that you need to have when it comes to everything in life.

CAUTION REQUIRED

It is only right at this time that I tell you that truly passionate people/candidates who love what they do love themselves. If you are going to take a risk, make sure that you place all the bets on yourself. It is so easy for people to get sidetracked and second guess who might be investing in them or not. We have all experienced at one time or another that feeling of hesitancy when we ask ourselves if we did everything that we should have done. After an interview, you might have thought of something you forgot to mention or left out. I do believe that there is way too much emphasis on people beating themselves up when it comes to the hiring process. All that does is cause the attention to be deferred to negative energy.

The job-searching process is challenging enough as it is, with its own level of stress. It is up to you to make it enjoyable. Remember that you are constantly building your brand. Always take note of what worked and what didn't work. As you do this, you will begin to see what areas need clarification so that you can make adjustments as needed. Don't overly discredit yourself. Always look at how much you've developed and the progress made, and just keep trying. Being challenged and knowing that there are areas in our lives that can be improved upon make us who we are. You will never know what you are capable of if you don't continuously stretch yourself.

❝ Being challenged and knowing that there are areas in our lives that can be improved upon make us who we are. You will never know what you are capable of if you don't continuously stretch yourself. ❞

Always go back and revisit the conversations that you had with past interviewers. Read over your notes, review their responses and any shared feedback on opportunity areas that you might address. Never beat yourself up over anything, even if it is a situation that turned out to be less than you expected. At the same time, be very cognizant of who you allow to speak to you and the group of people with whom you engage. All of your friends are not automatically equipped to provide professional insight. That statement holds true for some career counselors as well, in that many in this role have never recruited talent and may not readily relate to the high-paced demands of employers in this contingent, gig, fast-paced economy. Keep applying and learning.

MANNERS ARE IMPORTANT

The entire theme presented to you in *Rip the Resume* is how to go from average candidate to star candidate. It takes more than a mediocre attitude to do this, as you have clearly been shown. Competition is everywhere. Make it your number one priority to keep your name in the minds of people. This goes beyond just using general manners of a handshake or a courteous greeting. Those are important, and I am not taking anything away from these gestures, but there is more.

You might be thinking that manners are referring just to your everyday *please* and *thank you*. When it comes to the closing of the hiring process, you have to do what others won't do. Just what are the manners that are important when it comes to the end of the hiring process, when you have presented yourself in front of the hiring people?

Make it your business to understand the names of the individuals who you are meeting with, because you will need to have this information again. Be sure to use the proper salutation when it comes to addressing people by name. I want to advise you that the next 12 hours after an interview can definitely shift things in your favor, if you go straight from your interview to the nearest store and purchase a greeting card, add your own personal thoughtful message, and put it in the mail. Always rise above what you think might be the norm, and put extra effort into a complete finish. Let your efforts work for you.

Most candidates will run home and at some random point decide that it might benefit them to send a thank-you e-mail. By the way, they passed at least ten different stores on the way home with a selection of greeting cards that could have had a stamp placed on it and addressed to the appropriate person. How many candidates are sending a hand-written thank-you note? It takes the same amount of time, but two different efforts.

FOLLOW UP

Since you have already asked the hiring manager or recruiter what your next steps in the hiring process should be, as encouraged in Chapter 5, you should now have a follow-up date written down on a calendar. That is the reason why I shared with you the questions that you need to ask at the end of the interview: you can now set yourself up for what is to come next. Now you have your follow-up date. Whatever you have to do for this date to stand out, do it. This is the date on which you will reach out again to follow up.

A week after the initial follow-up date, do the same again, if appropriate. There is a great probability that hiring managers are still narrowing down the candidates they are interested in. You definitely want to know this! It is at this point that you will be able to ask if there is anything else that you need to do. As a matter of fact, this is where you ask if there is any additional information that is needed from you. The minute you are told to provide more information, stop everything and get on that immediately. Do not wait. You should be ready to send what is needed as soon as you find out what it is.

Eventually landed in D.C., sold hot sauce and jelly, just to make ends meet. Glamorous—not even close, but I knew my destiny wasn't locked in the position but in the promise of my remaining committed to the pursuit. I eventually landed at MCI.

GIVE 'EM THAT #BOOM 7

HASHTAGS, LIKES, AND POSTS

Let me circle back to everything I communicated to you in the first portion of this book with regard to your digital footprint. Aren't you glad that you cleaned up your social media presence? Everyone has social media accounts set up, but you have to use them so you have an upper hand. Leverage your social media in your job searches in addition to job boards and networking events to get in front of people.

The # sign is widely used in social communication and has become a popular way to uncover employers, hiring managers, and trending topics. Go to any social media platform and begin to positively and professionally exploit the power of the hashtag. While there, perform a few searches on the hashtag #toprecruiter, and you'll quickly uncover some of the powerful recruiting friends in my network who may be able to assist you in your search. (That tip alone was worth the price of the book.) You'll also see images and video of my crowning as the Season 4 Winner of *Top Recruiter*.

Here are four reasons why you should effectively utilize hashtags:

1. Hashtags in the most basic sense can be fun and self-serving.

2. Hashtags dramatically increase the reach of your posts, which means you'll get more exposure and hopefully more engagement and/or followers if you strategically use them.

3. Hashtags help you find businesses, employers, and people with similar interests.

4. Hashtags help you do market research to learn about your competitors, industry developments/movements, and business building opportunities.

The same is true when commenting, liking, and sharing posts. The challenge is trying to keep up with the algorithms these platforms use. Increasingly, they are working to minimize exposure. As a candidate, you have to find ways to interact with the brands that interest you and remain on their radar. Be proactive in learning about what the company is doing, and don't wait for new stuff to show up in your timeline, even if you follow the company or have it marked as a favorite. Visit the brand or company page or timeline specifically, so as to not miss the latest happenings.

APPLICANT TRACKING SYSTEMS

With the proliferation of recruiting tools, crawlers combing websites, off-shore agents scouring social media platforms and resume databases, now almost all companies use some form of applicant tracking system, referred to as ATS, as we have already mentioned. Companies use the ATS to house candidate resumes once they receive them. Companies also use the ATS to quickly do internal searches for talent by entering discipline, geography, industry, keywords, or some other parsing command.

This is important because as you craft your resume over time, you'll want to make sure you are using pertinent keywords that match your current or desired industry. I'm not suggesting you go overboard and just dump a dictionary's worth of words into your resume document. Rather, I want to remind you how important it is to use existing job descriptions and their contained language as you define the role you have or recently left. They are a solid barometer of what employers are looking for and will serve you well in the resume and power-prep process.

GITHUB AND ABOUT.ME

Broadcast yourself on About.me (generic appeal), and share who you are. Use GitHub if you are in the coding space. Reach out and refer to Knowem.com and research other social media platforms where you can secure your brand. For example, "Torin Ellis" is secured in places that are important to me. If you'd like to save your personal brand, do so. If it is already taken, consider an alternative that is available across much of the Internet. Again, the site Knowem.com will help you determine if a particular name or phrase is available on blogging platforms and social media sites.

KEEPING UP APPEARANCES

Remember how I mentioned my trips to the market in my casual clothes, much to the embarrassment of my daughters? Your brand includes your appearance at all times, but never is it as important as when you go to an interview. No interview prep guide would be complete without addressing this important factor of the job search process.

Everything leading up to and during the interview has been addressed, and the question now is: What do you wear? Sure, you can Google it to find out, and I'd suggest you do just that. But because some of you are still unsure in this cloud, startup, not-the-same-company-my-parents-worked-for economy, I thought it best to ask Joy Wansley and Opal Cooper of JoPal LLC how to approach proper dress. They shared their thoughts below. Have a read:

To begin, one needs a complete outfit that fits perfectly, comfortably, and exudes confidence. Style also begins from within: Good Hygiene, Strong Character, Good Posture, Confidence, and Clear Communication Skills. Remember your tone.

No matter the industry you are going into, there are standards for interview attire. Quick true story:

> *A young woman in her early 20s entered a work establishment with pajama bottoms and small curlers in her hair, wrapped up in a scarf with a button-front shirt. She may have been perfect for the position, but based on her attire, she missed out on an opportunity.*

Sounds crazy and, of course, you'd never dress like that. But assuming that khakis are appropriate because you see others wearing khakis may wind up costing you an opportunity just the same. As we share our contribution with Torin, we want your point of reference to always be on the side of caution. Always.

BASIC WARDROBE REFERENCE

Wardrobe Basic Pieces	
Male	**Female**
Suit: black, navy, or gray	Suit: black, navy, or gray
Blazer	Blazer
Khakis, basic slacks in black or navy	Pants/skirt
White/blue dress shirts, polo shirt	Blouses/shirts, solid or prints
Tie: solid or print	White/blue cotton/polyester blend button-collared shirts
Belt	Handbag: solid colors
Socks	Flesh-tone hosiery/opaque tights
Shoes: oxfords/loafers	Closed-toed pumps/kitten heels (1/2 inch or 1 inch in height)
Pair of jeans (dark wash)	Pair of jeans (dark wash)

For Women:

- Keep makeup natural
- Hair neatly styled or pulled away from your face
- Simple jewelry; nothing super big or flashy
- Manicured nails, clear polish, and minimal perfume

For Men:

- Hair neatly cut or pulled back
- Face clean shaven or beard and mustache trimmed
- Nails cleaned and trimmed, and minimal cologne or aftershave

What about color? It is not always about what you think looks best on you. Some colors can come across differently than others. So keep the following colors and meanings in mind:

- Black = strong, confident, dominant, overbearing
- Navy = friendly, calm, loyal, peaceful, steady, confident
- Red = confident, powerful, strong, stands out
- Grey = dull, basic, blends into the background
- Brown = humdrum, earthy, boring

In our opinion, the color navy is received as most friendly and least threatening. It looks good on everyone. But when all is said and done, the ultimate choice is yours.

Here is a quick chart on what NOT TO WEAR on interview day.

What NOT to Wear	
Male	**Female**
Ripped jeans	Above-the-knee-length skirts
Food-stained or wrinkled clothing	Low-cut tops
T-shirts	T-shirts
Visible piercings, i.e., nose, ear, tongue, lower lip	Spaghetti straps
Visible tattoos	Visible tattoos and piercings other than single earrings

I sat with JoPal LLC and closed our session with a few comments on creating a budget for a basic wardrobe. Keep in mind that this is an investment. There are a variety of ways to build your wardrobe without breaking the bank.

Look for sales, store coupons, and opportunities to shop online, where you often find deep discounts. Timing of sales shopping is everything. Consignment shops and thrift stores are another best-kept secret to find gently worn garments or suits for less than $50 and tops and bottoms for less than $4.99. You may even find brand new items if you're lucky and patient.

And last, but not least, everybody loves a party. How about a clothes swapping party? You can host a themed clothes swapping party and ask for specific garment pieces only. Invite your college friends or family members to your clothes swapping party, and watch your wardrobe get a makeover without costing you a dime.

We have given you tools to help you dress for success. No longer will you say, "I got the interview. Now what?" Always be ready to TAKE IT UP A NOTCH and stay true to your unique style. Always remember to create a style that PROMOTES YOU.

GIG/ON-DEMAND ECONOMY

Up until the year 2005 or so, the typical reference to people working for a company who were not full- or part-time employees was *temporary workers*. They were also referred to as *contingent workers*, especially as large recruiting firms and Vendor Management Systems became more common in the hiring process. Whether contingent or temporary, it meant the person working served as a supplement to the company's full- and part-time employee force to meet short-term business demands and labor needs. These employees served as cost-effective solutions for the company and were better for its bottom line.

Since about 2012, there has been a rise in what is referred to as the *gig economy*. A gig economy is an environment in which temporary positions are the standard, and the more common practice is to not hire employees but rather to contract with independent workers for these short-term engagements. These engagements can be found in nearly any industry these days, ranging from education, hospitality, and healthcare to errands, side projects, and professional services needed by companies of all sizes.

The trend toward a gig economy is in full swing, with imminent shifts in company-to-employee relationships becoming the norm for the foreseeable future. In fact, a study by Intuit predicted that by 2020, 40 percent of American workers would be independent contractors. A gig or on-demand economy focuses on those who freelance (professionally), akin to the business models of AirBnb and Uber using companies like Task Rabbit or the Upwork Community.

It is important to be aware of this trend because this economy, the rise of startups, shifts in innovation, and slow growth at companies like GE, IBM, Marriott, and others will require you to adapt how you go about your search. More important, it may factor into how you generate income while you search for that next role. Generating income might not be packaged in a traditional job and/or it may not happen during the hours of 9 to 5. Be prepared to shift if you have to; just be unwilling to make excuses or spend enormous amounts of time mired in a non-productive search.

If you want to see a cinematic portrayal of what I mean, watch the movie *The Pursuit of Happyness*. It is about entrepreneur Chris Gardner (played by Will Smith), who was a homeless salesman refusing to quit despite all his struggles. He was trying to create a better life for his son. In Gardner's story, you will see many of the things that I have told you about. He took many losses, but he never stopped and always found a way to make his disadvantages work for him. Ultimately, he got the position he was pursuing, but he had to find other ways to make it happen first.

Learned the game of interviewing, walked in my purpose, and built one of the top-ranked teams in the country. That launched my entrepreneurial career because even there, I wasn't respected and do not advocate that any employee works where he or she isn't appreciated.

BEFORE WE GO . . . 8

BIASES AND DIVERSITY

"DIVERSITY IS MENTAL IN ORIGIN AND MANIFESTS IN WHO WE ARE, HOW WE ARE PERCEIVED OR SEEN, AND IN ALL THAT WE DO. DIVERSITY IS BEAUTIFUL, CURIOUS, AND NOT AFRAID TO MINGLE WITH THE UNKNOWN." ~ t:ell

This brings me to the subject of biases and diversity. It is very important to me for many reasons. I remember, for example, a man who was adamant about my NOT stepping into his yard to deliver the newspaper or to collect the money he owed when I delivered newspapers in Iowa as a teen. I remember reporting how he threatened me, a 13- or 14-year-old, and how the company I worked for said absolutely nothing in my defense. This is not at all what any young person or adult should have to experience, but it happens.

Even today, we have story after story highlighting the lack of diversity in the tech space or the inherent biases that have prevented talented people from securing opportunities and/or moving up within company ranks. We are on the cusp of a major shift in terms of workplace and racial demographics. In the next five years, millennials will represent just about half of all people in the workplace, and by 2030, black and brown people will become the majority here in the United States.

These shifts are important, as they will impact and reflect who is in charge, shape the composition of our workplaces, and ultimately either highlight the incredible companies that we are building or show the vulnerability of building productive and strong teams. I've never seen the value in not having inclusion, and I can't possibly see how it will serve any of us in the future.

I've been recruiting for a long time for all kinds of organizations—sales, telecom, IT, software, Fortune 500, startups—and when you look at their sales and technical teams, at their board of directors, and at their leadership, diversity has always been negligible. As a Human Capital Strategist, I connect organizations with top diversity professionals by establishing search strategies that identify the people and practices that will help the company better deliver and produce results. I feel obligated to mention this very important topic since many of you will soon be in leadership positions, holding directorships, and working side by side with others who are different. Simply put, *diversity* means a difference between you and me, and that difference should propel our efforts toward meeting a common objective.

Diversity begins with thought, it involves an organization's culture and its people, and it includes everything else in between. There are plenty of residual benefits that can occur for and within a firm that embraces a solid diversity initiative, but the challenge has long been making sure the business case is clearly made. It has typically been hard for companies to define what an effective workforce diversity initiative looks like, even though efforts have been made to do so for more than a generation. Yet, I'm encouraged by this generation. I believe that many of you feel as I do, which is if the leadership doesn't buy into a strong diversity initiative, then none of the talking matters. It becomes window dressing.

"Diversity begins with thought, it involves an organization's culture and its people, and it includes everything else in between."

Take California's Silicon Valley, for example. Beginning back in 2013 and continuing through most of 2015, the lack of diversity problem was brought into the forefront. When hiring reports were released to the public, the world's trailblazing technology companies came up sorely lacking in gender and ethnic diversity. To date, the diversity problem continues to be an area of concern, even as these companies have made strides by simply acknowledging the issue. However, while many of these companies have diversity and inclusion statements on their website and have individuals in diversity and inclusion roles, there just hasn't been a lot of movement in that area. (We could have looked at a number of other industries and found the same, if not worse, absence of representation.)

That's not to suggest these companies haven't been trying; it's more a matter of having the kitchen in order. So in remaining true to who I am and seeing how much I care about you and the workplaces that my children and your children will have to frequent, I want to see progress being made—now and into the future. I want the word *diversity* to be well-received and not seen as another toxic disparity between people who are different from the people in power. Because you will soon be leaders and decision makers, here's what is important if you want to build a foundation for stronger diversity in the workplace:

1. A truly strong initiative
2. A tie-in business case that answers: "Why does this make sense?"
3. Direction and resources from leadership or the founder(s) of the organization

Without these three components, any diversity initiative is going to be nothing more than another press release and some window dressing. Truthfully, you don't necessarily know that a certain plan is going to be effective, but you do know that you've put forth a valiant effort in trying to make sure it is genuine, thoughtful and strategic in scope and that people are serious about approaching the desired mission and result.

One company that seems to be getting it right is Intel. When the diversity issue became apparent to Intel CEO Brian Krzanich, he took a big and bold lead in saying, "We have to do something about this." The company followed through. In 2015, a five-year, $300-million global diversity and inclusion initiative was put into place that resulted in Intel exceeding its diverse hiring goals and meeting its diverse talent retention goals it set for the first year of implementation.

In order to put together a diversity initiative that makes sense, you need to include a variety of people from a variety of levels inside of your organization. You need to be thoughtful and willing to explore—push, even—boundaries of the past. Through that effort, I believe you can develop a successful diversity strategy. The sooner this mindset is in place, the better, which is why I'm taking the time to share this with you now. We have Fortune 50 companies—still—that have a severe lack of diversity. That means they've ignored the issue of diversity for what, … *decades*? Or is it that they haven't been successful in their efforts to address it for decades? It starts with the thought. Companies have to acknowledge that lack of representation is an issue, and many are beginning to seriously do that.

I remember working with Be The Match, a nonprofit organization, based in Minneapolis, MN, that is a global leader in bone marrow transplantation. At the time, Be The Match was trying to reach a diverse audience. One form of outreach involved putting up posters at historically black colleges and universities. The posters highlighted a phenomenal message featuring people that were all Caucasian. And for some time, they were monitoring the response and didn't understand why the numbers were low and barely moving in terms of new interest. They learned that the posters didn't resonate with the students. It took the organization years to realize why they were not receiving a lot of action through their poster campaigns. It was because people would walk by the poster and not respond to it.

Once you get into a role or as you are vying for a role, you have to recognize that your biases may creep into the process of how you build relationships with peers, interview talent in the future, read over resumes, frame questions, evaluate responses, mentor and receive mentorship, and lead; and in all of the additional how-to modems of business. I caution you to remember the wider landscape of talent that exists and to check your biases so they do not paralyze progress. While at MCI Communications, I was leading one of the top and most successful sales teams in the country. I had a director who said, "We can't trust a man with hair on his face." He was referring to my short, well-kept, shadow of a beard similar to the one I wear today. Despite having proven myself, this particular director was clinging to his bias and never gave me the full benefit of consideration I thought I had earned.

There exists religious diversity, political diversity, and age and gender diversity. There's also educational, geographical, relationship-related, parental, and industry-related diversity. With so many triggers, the issue of diversity is important enough for me to include in a book targeting career development and job search tactics. It encompasses a broad spectrum, and you have to be willing to tackle the issue for what it's worth in your particular environment. The bottom line is: diversity is absolutely important, no matter who or where you are, but the strategy will always look different for every organization.

A FEW LAST WORDS

I spend a significant amount of my time answering and generating e-mails and fielding and making phone calls, which often results in my simply being of service. I spend hours performing research, preparing for speaking engagements, radio segments, and meetings, and I do that because I care about my craft. I do it because I care about the candidate experience. The candidate experience has always been at the core of the work I've done . . . always.

And while there are a number of human resource employees, hiring managers, and recruiting personnel who will ignore you or lead you down a rabbit hole of disappointment, I don't want you to become disgusted with the interviewing process. There are a number of reasons why these bad experiences happen. Many of them are controllable, but they still happen. With the introduction of even more technology in the years to come, I suspect the experience will suffer even more before it gets better. Stay dialed in; don't check out. And don't lump everyone you encounter during the job search process in the "bad bucket" because of a previous negative experience.

It strikes me as important that our needs in our personal and professional life change over time. For as long as the interview has been with us, it is still a demanding and scary part of the hiring process for some. The need for this book was apparent, and I had to develop an easy read that you could refer to over and over again as you grow your career. Remember a solid job search strategy revolves around a 20/20/60 job hunting plan.

- 20% of your time on job boards
- 20% of your time on social media
- 60% of your time networking/referrals

A job hunting plan requires a performance-based resume, an understanding of how recruiters find candidates, and applying through the backdoor. Networking (60%) is the key to the backdoor. It represents much of what you need to do.

The aim of drafting *Rip the Resume* and hosting on-campus boot camps is to imbue each undergraduate, alumni, or tenured professional with active knowledge. The formula for a great job search changes from industry to industry, role to role, and person to person. The prescription that I've rendered is not the only way to address the desired scenario, but rather a trusted compilation of experience over time. It has been tested and proven to be effective. And with recruiters feeling as though 60% of undergraduates are unprepared for the position, the least you can do is come prepared, showing that you're taking your search seriously. You want to place companies and hiring managers in a position that reinforces their trust in you.

The only way to enjoy true success is to go through the experience. It is similar to the flashy automobile you see on Instagram: it looks great on an iPhone, but it would probably look even better in front of your spot. I know my editor knows what *spot* is (*smiling*). In closing, you are going to get dirty in the job search process—most likely, the process will not go as smoothly as you envision. Take your lumps, learn from them, and arrive even more prepared for the next conversation.

As a matter of fact, I want to hear from you. I want you to visit the Rip The Resume website (***www.riptheresume.com***) and share your interview stories with me. Over the next several months, I'll review the various submitted stories and segment them into consistent themes. At some point, I'll reach out to some of you to discuss your unique situation and provide you with a complimentary personal session that better prepares you for a future interview. While on the site, poke around for additional articles, blog posts, and resources that should be of value.

Tell a friend to tell a friend to grab the book and do the same. Look out for how you might be part of *Rip the Resume II.*

I have so much more in store for you. Remember, let your light shine bright as to who you are. *Rip the Resume!*

Resources

As my final gift to you, I thought I would share some valuable resources with you as you begin (or continue) your job search with a new perspective and, I hope, reignited enthusiasm. To begin, the following individuals contributed invaluable advice and expertise as I created *Rip the Resume*. Consider allowing them to help you as well.

RESUME WRITER

Chris Fields, MLHR
Resume Crusade, www.resumecrusade.com
Instagram @cd_fields
Twitter @new_resource

STYLE CONSULTANTS

JoPal LLC
The Fusion of Style & Education
Joy Wansley & Opal Cooper
Instagram @2Jopal
Twitter @Jopal2Jopal
jopal757@gmail.com
757-785-5725

TECHNOLOGY RESOURCES

In the job search landscape, you will find that much of the technology is geared toward the employer and that you are rarely ever made aware of it. Unlike social media, much of the technology sits behind the curtain, but it exists. It exists to increase efficiency, to make better matches, to lower recruiting costs, to hire more engaged candidates, to project future productivity, to determine potential leaders, and I could go on. For the most part, technology is positive and renders positive implications. With all of the changes in the past decade, from candidate assessments and job boards to blind testing and referral systems, many suggest that recruiting is ripe for a major disruption.

Having this insight into the role and types of technology involved in the process is good for you. This knowledge allows you to be aware of the factors that might extend your search or minimize your effectiveness in securing a promotion or new job. Just as you wouldn't dare purchase a Sunday newspaper to look for employment today, it is as important to know what not to do this time next year. (Which reminds me, augmented and virtual reality are on the scene and will play a role in your job search within the next 24 months.)

And while some of the technologies will go and new solutions will be ushered in, there are indisputable aspects that will never change in this process. No matter what anyone tells you, no matter what report or white paper is published, *people* do the best job of hiring people. At some point, people must communicate with one another. Technology aside, never let your communication skills become rusty. Don't get caught slipping.

That being said, explore and take advantage of the technology that's out there for you. You probably recognize some of the mobile app names from their website counterparts, but you may also discover some new avenues to enhance your job search.

JOB BOARDS/SEARCH ENGINES

Indeed Job Search

At a glance, Indeed Job Search appears to be a rather straightforward job search app. Just like the full website, the iPhone app lets users search for jobs and filter the results based on industry, location, desired salary, and more. The Indeed app aggregates listings from thousands of sources, including other online job boards, company career pages, and newspaper classifieds. Users can set up email alerts to be notified when new jobs appear in a specific category. When you find a job you like, save it so you can apply later, or attach your resume to your account so you can apply in-app.

· ·

Jobs by CareerBuilder

With the Jobs by CareerBuilder app, you can search for jobs by industry, location, or company. You don't even need a CareerBuilder account to use the app: Simply upload your resume from your smart device or Dropbox account, and start your search. You can track and view your job search history, save jobs for later, and even view your competition with average stats on other applicants' education levels and years of experience. CareerBuilder will also recommend jobs and alert you when your application has been received and viewed.

LinkedIn Job Search

LinkedIn Job Search is easily one of the most popular professional networking tools out there, but it isn't just about selling yourself with a flattering personal profile. Just like on the LinkedIn website, LinkedIn Job Search lets you search for open positions in your industry and sort them by date posted, salary, and other criteria. When you find something you like, you can apply directly in-app with your LinkedIn profile. The app will also recommend jobs based on your profile and past search criteria, and it will notify you when a relevant job goes live in your area.

LinkUp (http://www.linkup.com)

When you're searching for positions on open job boards, you run the risk of applying to a fake or scam job. The LinkUp job search engine pulls listings directly from company websites, so the jobs you find through the app are always current and legitimate. Like many other job-hunting apps, this one lets you save listings you like, revisit your search history, and receive alerts for relevant jobs.

Monster Job Search

The Monster Job Search app is a mobile companion to one of the biggest online job boards. Like competing apps, it lets you search for new openings and filter your results based on your needs and preferences. Sign in to your Monster account to access your uploaded resumes, cover letters, and previously submitted job applications. You can also sign up to be notified when new positions are listed.

Simply Hired

Like Indeed Job Search, the Simply Hired app is an aggregation tool that gathers job listings from a big variety of sources, including other job boards and company websites. The app also lets you set up email alerts for new listings based on your search criteria. By subscribing to a particular job category on both Simply Hired and Indeed.com, you can minimize the chances of missing a new opportunity in your field. Save jobs you like so you can apply later, or apply in-app if you already uploaded your resume.

Switch

When you work in the tech industry, switching jobs can be a real hassle, especially if the wrong person at your current company finds out. Keep the heat down with Switch, an anonymous job search app that lets employed tech professionals quietly search for new positions. The interface, which resembles dating app Tinder, allows you to "swipe" right on positions you're interested in. Hiring managers will see only your professional profile—not your name or contact information—and if they like what they see, you'll instantly be connected so you can chat further about the opening.

SALARY EVALUATORS

Career Bliss (*www.careerbliss.com*)

CareerBliss is an online community designed to help professionals find happiness in their career and workplace. To that end, it offers its members access to 3.5 million job postings, 4 million salaries, and thousands of company reviews. Its interface allows users to engage and evaluate multiple user-generated data points such as job satisfaction, pay scale, and overall employee happiness, known as the "Bliss-Score," that can help users to compare careers or help determine if a particular job is a good fit.

Payscale.com—(*www.payscale.com*)

Payscale.com's mission is to provide employees and employers with accurate compensation information. The company boasts its use of crowdsourcing and big data technologies to develop the world's largest database of salary profiles. With this information, employees can find out exactly what they should be paid, and employers can be updated on competitive pay rates. Other services include a free salary and benefits report, career planning assistance, and location-based cost of living research.

Aequitas

The Aequitas mobile app provides users with access to current wage data, interview, resume-building and salary negotiation tools. It offers information about wages and the Equal Pay Act and connects users to equal pay-related social networks/discussions. The application is both iPhone and iPad accessible.

NETWORKING

CityHour

If you're just getting started in or want to move up in your field, many career experts recommend setting up informal meetings with industry professionals to learn more about their career experiences. Eliminate the awkward "ask" phase with CityHour, an app that syncs with your LinkedIn profile to find contacts who are already open to scheduling in-person meetings. You can quickly connect and schedule a meeting with anyone in a 50-mile (80 kilometers) radius, and once you've selected a meeting place, the information is automatically synced with your phone's calendar.

Intro

Intro by about.me isn't a job-listing app, but it does help you network with people in your industry by turning your about.me page into a digital business card. You can control what you share—your page, phone number, email, or all of the above—and keep track of the cards you send and receive. Found someone who might be useful in your job search? View that person's about.me page in the app, and save his or her information right to your phone's contacts.

Reach

With the Reach app by Big Rock Labs, finding local professionals and events in your industry has never been easier. Once you're logged in through your LinkedIn account or email address, you can search for nearby users with your phone's GPS sensor or for users who have checked in to specific nearby locations. If you find someone you want to connect with, "Reach Out" by sending a request. If the person accepts, contact information for the two of you is exchanged, and you can start a productive conversation. You can also discover trending events near you and register to attend in-app.

TOOLS AND ORGANIZATION

Jobaware

The highest-rated iOS job search app, Jobaware allows you to sync all your job search activity on the web and on the app, as well as integrate with LinkedIn. You can track your search progress, compare jobs in different cities, check specific companies for jobs, and view salary information. The app also connects you with a variety of learning resources to aid in your job search. The service is also available online (*www.jobaware.com/jobs*).

. . . .

JobCompass (*www.jobcompass.net*)

When you're considering a new job opening, proximity is key. Accepting a position that's far from home could mean you'll have to move or endure a long commute. The JobCompass website and app focuses on finding you jobs that are nearby. While most job boards allow you to filter search results based on your ZIP code, the JobCompass app uses your smartphone's GPS to show you where the job is in relation to you or another specified location. If you're thinking about moving to a new area, search for jobs in more than 55 countries to see what's out there. And when you find a job you like, e-mail it yourself or apply directly within the app.

About the Author

"Predominately white, Asian, and male."

An apt description of the current workforce found in tech companies around the country.

Torin Ellis, Human Capital Strategist based in Baltimore, MD, aims to change the face of the American workforce.

"Tech companies are at the forefront of the diversity conversation," says Ellis.

But the issue is much larger than that industry alone. His thoughts are that ALL companies must embrace diversity and inclusion initiatives that have the support of leadership.

Ellis, 47, was born in Florida and raised in the Midwest, spending time in Ohio, Indiana, and Iowa. He joined the Air Force in 1987 and served as a communications analyst while stationed in the Philippines and Texas.

He left the service in 1990 and worked for Union Pacific Railroad and Marshall Fields before joining MCI in 1993. While at the telecommunications giant, he sold long-distance, paging, and toll-free services to small business customers. In his first year, he averaged more than 200% above his sales quota and was promoted to lead a sales team.

In 1998, the entrepreneurial spirit called Ellis to go out on his own. He formed a recruiting company, and he has been contracted by such firms as Verizon Wireless, Oracle, AOL, Expedient, ESPN, Redfin, and others to find qualified employees.

Over the years, Ellis has placed hundreds of workers. "About 20 percent of those positions filled were in the engineering/technical arena," he says. "The rest were in executive, sales, and sales leadership positions."

Ellis had been contracted by Monster.com to be a part of their traveling speaking team, and he's also been hired to speak at the Department of Labor's "Youth Opportunity" programs all around the country. Through these engagements, Ellis has spoken to thousands of students and professionals.

Ellis is featured in the documentary film "Top Recruiter," which can be found online (*www.toprecruiter.tv*) and is the Season 4 winner.

Ellis operates a recruitment marketing and talent attraction firm focused on diversity. His firm serves as a hybrid between the marketing and recruiting functions that are often disjointed or ignored in contingency firms and too pricey for most companies, when considering retained firms. This results in clients being treated more like a partner in the process.

Ellis says diversity is a buzzword that carries different meanings for different people.

"I want to sit in the space of positivity. I want to work with CEOs and C-suite executives to address the issue with creative solutions that increase representation (those who are black, brown, women, or disabled) and support the bottom-line."

NOTES

NOTES

NOTES

NOTES

NOTES

NOTES

NOTES

NOTES

NOTES

NOTES